SELLING LUXURY HOMES

SELLING LUXURY HOMES

BECOME THE PREFERRED REAL ESTATE AGENT AND TRUSTED ADVISOR TO HIGH-END CLIENTS IN YOUR MARKET

John Cotton, Jr.

Published by Tide-mark Press, Ltd.
Windsor, Connecticut

Printed and bound in the United States
First Edition

Library of Congress Cataloging-in-publication Data
Cotton, John, Jr.
Selling Luxury Homes

ISBN 978-1-594906923

Library of Congress Control Number
2010929895

To my fellow Realtors®

*Through hard work,
persistence and professionalism,
you make a challenging profession
look easy*

CONTENTS

CONTENTS

ACKNOWLEDGMENTS

LIKE MANY PROJECTS OR ENDEAVORS I HAVE UNDERTAKEN, THE WRITing of this book turned out to be way more involved then I would have ever dreamed. During the 18 months it took to complete the work, it began at a somewhat leisurely, measured pace. As the work took shape, it became an all-consuming, full-time job.

There are so many people without whom the book could not have been completed. I list them here with my heart-felt gratitude.

Kyle Conners was immensely helpful in editing my first draft. We would get together to discuss his questions on content I had created. Other times he "interviewed" me from one of my outlines to create content. His questions forced me to clarify and explain things that seemed obvious to me but probably would not be to a reader. Thanks Kyle.

If writing 60,000 words wasn't hard enough, try coming up with 400 impactful words for the front and back cover. I first turned to self-publishing guru Dan Poynter (www.parapublishing.com) who happened to be traveling throughout Southeast Asia during my inquiries. He never failed to send email answers to my queries at untold hours from all over the globe. He was extremely generous with his time. He put me in touch with two great people who made a huge difference in the quality of this book.

Susan Kendrick of Write To Your Market (www.writetoyourmarket.com) was phenomenal in honing my title and subtitle and back cover copy. Dan also suggested Barbara McNichol (www.BarbaraMcNichol.com) as my final draft editor. Her painstaking review of each word, endless questions, and rewrites benefit you, the reader, in ways you'll never know.

Writing the Internet and social networking chapters especially challenged me as they constantly evolve in their relevance to luxury real estate marketing. Gratitude goes to Dan Kompass (www.webblotter.com), my own webmaster and web guru. Matthew Ferraara (www.MatthewFerrara.com), the undisputed expert on all things dealing with social networking for real estate agents, also generously gave me his time. My chapter on social networking was created largely from talking to Matthew. He honed my manuscript into what I think is an immensely helpful chapter on social networking.

I asked Ed Primeau (www.primeauproductions.com) to supplement my information on social media. In addition, Curt Warner (www.platinum-salesystems.com) was enthusiastic about this book from the beginning. He contributed immensely to the section on individual property websites.

As I mentioned, much of the book was dictated into a digital recorder with a voice file emailed to Keith at eWord Solutions (www.eWordSolutions.com). Keith's team transcribes and turns around near-perfect Word documents, usually by the time the sun rises on the East Coast the following morning.

When this book was nearing completion, I showed the cover art to various experts with whom I was consulting. Without exception, each one raved about the cover design done by Andrew Newman (www.newmandesign.com) Working from his low-key Cape Cod office, Andrew has become a true master of design.

Scott Kaiser of Tidemark Press (www.tide-mark.com) published my first book, *A Dog's Guide to Life*. Although it was written on purpose, it was published by accident because of Scott's enthusiasm. It only seemed natural to return to Scott for help in publishing this book.

Lastly, I need to express my gratitude for the love and support of my family including my four kids, Melissa, Andrew, Maxwell, and Alexa, and most of all my supportive wife, Anne Marie. Aside from being a great proofreader, whenever she hears one of my ideas for a new project, she always says, "You can do that."

With heartfelt thanks and love, I express gratitude to all these people and especially to my family.

SELLING LUXURY HOMES

INTRODUCTION

WHAT WOULD IT BE LIKE TO SELL A MULTIMILLION-DOLLAR PROPerty? How would it feel to gain a spectacular listing and meet the accomplished people who either own that property or have the ability to purchase?

For most agents, such wonderment passes as quickly as thoughts of winning the lottery. Although some earn $500,000 or more a year, few earn that much on one transaction. Thoughts like "I could never do that, or "I wasn't born into that sphere of influence," or "I don't travel in the right circles," or "I don't know the right people" snatch away the dream. Such self-defeating beliefs can keep agents stuck in the classic story about the outsider looking in.

I confess. I have felt like an outsider. I was able to break out of that "story" and succeed in luxury real estate because when I started this career at age twenty-one, I didn't know "it couldn't be done." I was lucky. No one told me anything was impossible, so I believed I could succeed—and did! The firm I started in my college dorm room grew to become one of the most respected real estate companies on Cape Cod. During more than three decades in this business, I have been involved in nearly every record-breaking residential sale on Cape Cod, either as agent or coach to the agent involved.

Many agents not only have negative perceptions of what they can sell and accomplish, but they take an extra step. They surround themselves with people who only too willingly reinforce the notion that success in high-end real estate won't work for them.

Understand the Mindset

You'll find that this book helps you understand the mindset you need to succeed in this stratum of the real estate business. It also provides specific techniques and plans of action to launch you on the path to being a luxury real estate expert.

Just as important as adjusting your own mindset is understanding the mindsets of those individuals you desire to serve. To assist you, Chapter 2 pinpoints the four categories of wealthy individuals—WANNAs, KINDAs, REALLYs and SUPERs—and how they think. As important as adjusting your own mindset, we must also understand the mindset of the high net worth individuals we desire to serve.

In addition, Chapter 4 explains ways to find high-end buyers and sellers, and how to provide useful information these individuals crave. Becoming a primary source for them builds the perception of you as a market expert in your chosen high-end niche.

Your next step is to become a trusted advisor to the wealthy—one who's called on time and again for expert advice about the market. You can assist them as they monitor their positions of wealth and make the necessary plans to maintain, preserve, and conserve that wealth. This will put you at the epicenter of the sphere of experts they access for various aspects of their financial lives. Your ultimate goal? Preeminence in the field of luxury real estate.

What's Your Price Range?

Let's say luxury real estate is defined as the top 10% of the market. (Look for more on definitions in Chapter 1.) Do luxury real estate specialists exclude listings or sales below a certain price level? Should you pass them on or refer out properties that don't meet that definition?

My philosophy has always been to treat *all* potential clients like a million dollars, regardless of the price range of their properties. Throughout my 36-year career, I have never discriminated based on the price of a listing or a particular buyer. The following story illustrates why.

IT STARTED WITH A SALE UNDER $150,000

A couple on the young side of middle age walked into our office one day. New to the area, they'd heard about our Village and all its amenities. They wanted to look at the available homes. At the time it was possible to find homes in the Village for under $200,000. Soon the couple purchased a home for $131,500—not a luxury transaction by most people's definition. We soon discovered they were holding out on us in terms of their financial power.

That same year, they decided to buy a condo for one of their parents and closed on their selected choice for $290,000—still not a luxury property but getting better.

After enjoying the ambience and charm of the Village for not even a year, they decided to buy a waterfront home for $859,000 that showed signs of age and disrepair. While this property was approaching the category of "luxury," the dwelling itself was in such poor condition, they razed it and had a highly regarded architect design a beautiful new home. They began constructing it using the highest standards.

When the home was nearing completion, a disagreement with a neighbor ensued over the refuse company noisily emptying the construction dumpster in predawn hours. The next day, the owners decided this wasn't the neighborhood for them, and they began looking at other properties.

In short order, they bought a waterfront home that anyone would define as "luxury" at $3,475,000. Even though it was in perfect condition, they made major renovations. About the same time, my agency sold the new house they never moved into for $1,600,000.

After several years living in this home, they decided to buy another in a waterfront town some distance away and sold their latest home for $4,450,000. Before long, the purchaser of that home decided to move on, and our agency sold the home again for $5,198,000.

The new buyers enjoyed the home for several years, then decided the location wasn't for them. Our agency helped them find and purchase a nearby property for $12,500,000 that required extensive modernization and renovation.

This entire chain of transactions that began with a couple who some assume had modest means, purchasing a non-luxury home for $131,500. Wealthy people don't always tip their hand right off. See how this purchase multiplied into multimillion-dollar sales?

Many agents would have jumped into this chain of sales at the $3 million mark. In fact, some tried but were unsuccessful. The people came to know and trust us, so they weren't motivated to change.

They could just as easily have been a couple who could only afford a $200,000 property when they first visited. After all, being able to purchase a $200,000 second home puts you at the top of the income/ net worth strata. Many of our clients began as purchasers in the lower end of the price scale and moved up as their financial situation grew.

THE DECISION IS YOURS

You can specialize in a certain price range or go with my philosophy to treat everyone like a million dollars regardless of their price range. I prefer to list and sell homes in all ranges so I can "pay the bills," and when the mega-sales come along, I bank all the fees. If I can be successful doing this, so can you.

Welcome to the world of luxury real estate and learning how to make it yours. Let's begin.

LUXURY REAL ESTATE
DEFINED

IF YOU ASK PEOPLE TO DEFINE "LUXURY" REAL ESTATE, YOU'LL GET many different answers. A number of people may say $1 million and above, but in some markets, $1 million would be the price of a starter home. Others may think "luxury" pricing begins at $10 million. Depending on the market and location, either of these answers could be correct.

In the Hamptons outside of Manhattan, or in Hawaii or parts of California, the definition of luxury could begin at $5 million. On Cape Cod, it starts at $1 million. How perfect; I love round numbers.

In some places, people may believe that only homes over a certain size or in certain locations, such as on the water or a mountainside, qualify as luxury real estate. In other places, homes without wheels might fit that qualification!

Another way to define luxury real estate is to add a zero to the average price of properties you're currently listing or selling.

My two preferred ways to define luxury real estate for any market are these:

(1) top 20% of listings, or

(2) top 10% in actual sales calculated by price.

Here's an example of the first way. In my market—Cape Cod, Massachusetts—3,317 homes are listed for sale at the time of this writing. Now, 20% of 3,317 is 664, so the top 20% of listings would mean the top 664 homes listed from lowest to highest price. In this case, any property priced at $1,100,000 would be qualified as luxury.

Alternatively, the top 10% of 2,627 actual sales from the previous 12 months are calculated the same way and result in an approximate cutoff point of $700,000.

In a stronger market where the supply and demand is more equally balanced, these two numbers—$1,100,000 and $700,000—are often closer together. However, for use throughout this book, let's define "luxury" real estate as the second option—the top 10% of sales in any given market.

Certain publications and web sites that feature "luxury" homes maintain minimum prices for properties they list. These may or may not coincide with your chosen definition, so first establish a standard in your own business. Use a definition that's appropriate for your markets and can provide you with a cutoff number.

Why Determine a Cutoff Number?

But you may be asking this question: Why determine a cutoff number if you adopt my philosophy and treat everyone like a million-dollar buyer regardless of the price point? Because devoting a higher level of marketing to properties that qualify as "luxury" is justified, given the higher expectation of the seller and the fee you stand to earn.

Be aware, of course, that no matter how you define "luxury" real estate, the number of individuals who can buy or sell these properties is limited. Obviously, $1,000,000-dollar-and-up properties aren't as plentiful as $200,000 homes. The good news? High-end buyers often own two or more homes, making it worth your while to cultivate lasting relationships with them.

Disadvantages of High-End Real Estate

If you specialize in high-end versus low-end real estate, your fees are higher but most likely the number of transactions you complete is smaller. Plus if you list and sell dozens of lesser-priced homes, it's not as painful when one transaction fails.

On the other hand, if a $5 million sale falls apart, many months of hard work can be lost. To make matters worse, you might not have a significant number of other transactions in the pipeline to make up the shortfall.

If you're in a seasonal or second-home market such as Cape Cod, it's important to understand that someone purchasing a property as a second home—even for the lowest price available in your market—is probably in the top 5% of income earners. As with the couple in the Introduction, these buyers tend to upgrade regularly, so keeping them as clients for life is highly desirable. Yet doing so takes focused time and effort.

Seasonality in any location can lead to longer marketing periods. In markets such as Cape Cod or Florida, for example, properties are more likely to sell at certain times of the year. Cape Cod buyers come out in early spring and autumn. In Florida, an uptick of buyers usually occurs during the winter months. Therefore, if a property comes on the market outside the prime season, you can be looking at a longer sales cycle than for lower-priced properties. This fact— combined with the need to produce elaborate brochures, web sites, and advertising—means that high-end real estate can be expensive to list and market. (Refer to the discussion on the need for long listing contracts in Chapter 7.)

Besides the additional marketing expense, luxury properties take a long time to show because they're bigger and more detailed than non-luxury ones. It can take an entire day to show only two or three high-end properties. And although transactions for luxury homes tend to stay together until closing, they may take months or some- times years to arrange. When a high-end sale falls through, the time you've invested can be impossible to make up.

Benefits of the Luxury Market:
Great Houses, High Fees, Cool People
Despite the downsides, the benefits of being a luxury real estate specialist outweigh having many transaction eggs in one basket.

For one, financing can be easier because many times buyers pay cash. Even if they're obtaining a loan, they typically only make one phone call to their private banker to secure it, giving the transaction every appearance of being a cash deal.

Also, high-end transactions rarely fall apart. Wealthy individuals tend to be more in tune with the buying process because they're buying their second or third residence. Having been through this many times before, they're experienced buyers.

GREAT HOUSES

I've observed that luxury homes have one of two emotional "tugs" buyers use to justify their purchases. For some, buying a luxury home is a just representation of their success and a reward for their achievements. For others, owning a great house in a spectacular location pulls their families together, especially important if family members have drifted apart over the years.

Buyers who can afford a great house are obviously successful. If they didn't inherit wealth, they got to this point by working hard and sacrificing a good deal of family time—missing their children's plays and sports games, family dinners, and so on.

Purchasing a great house often enables these buyers to recapture time they've lost getting to where they were able to afford it. They might say something like, "I need to pull my family together again, and this property is the magnet to do just that."

EMOTIONAL REWARDS FOR ALL

While I was at a buyer's house for which he paid $3 or $4 million, the new owner told me, "You know what? The funniest thing happened. My son came for the weekend and he stayed for six weeks. And he's talking about getting a job here next summer. This is the best investment I've ever made."

How striking! Caught up in the emotion of his son getting a job and staying the whole summer, this buyer's heartfelt conclusion was, "Why didn't we buy a house here sooner?"

And that's the exciting part of the business for me. I feel rewarded seeing the smile on people's faces when that occurs. Sometimes, they weren't aware that could be an outcome when they first looked for a luxury home.

Every morning, I wake up in my own home situated on five acres with a distant river view. I look around with pride at my surroundings and think back to the modest home on a quarter acre that was my childhood residence.

Later in the day, I go on an appointment at a 12,000-square-foot home that has elevators, 15 baths, tiled garage floors, and electronics that cost more than my entire property. Returning to my home on those days allows me to rediscover the concept of relativity. More often than not, I undertake another expensive project.

I find it a special treat to see many incredible examples of craftsmanship as well as original artwork I once saw through heavy eyelids in slideshows during art history class. More than once, I have come home and wanted to tear my house apart and start over. But then I remember, I've created a happy home that I can afford. Although I'm not as rich as my clients, I realize I do have great wealth!

HIGH FEES
What benefit do most agents expect to gain by selling luxury real estate? Obviously, it's earning higher fees than for non-luxury homes.

I won't mention specific fees, but I assure you that, as a rule, selling fees for high-end homes tend to be larger—much larger—than most. Although many agents make $500,000 a year selling real estate, few have made $500,000 on one transaction. Holding that half-million-dollar commission check is exciting, I can assure you—if for no other reason than the well-earned extreme sense of accomplishment that far exceeds the dollar amount.

Many luxury real estate professionals agree that it is no harder to sell a $5 million property than it is to sell one valued at one tenth that amount. For all transactions, the trick is to get the listing, find the right buyer, and negotiate the best transaction.

The actual selling part, though, can be easier with high-end real estate. I have found that decisions to buy a high-end home can be made impulsively, and occasionally after only one or two showings. Also, I can assure you I've never had to measure closets, investigate the BTU output of the furnace, or chase down the R factor of the bulkhead doors in a multimillion-dollar home.

Many agents eyeing the high-end market ask: "Do I have to cut my fee or charge a lower fee on a multimillion-dollar home sale?" Not necessarily. High-end sellers know that with luxury properties the stakes are higher and expenses greater, and the expertise is more valuable and therefore costly. (Look for a discussion on fee preservation in Chapter 19: The Three Negotiation Strategies You Need in the High End.)

Cool People

Odds are, those who can afford one or more multimillion-dollar homes have an interesting story and are unique individuals. I can think of no other career in which I could have interacted with such high-caliber professionals or corporate chieftains when in my late twenties. It can be both astounding and inspirational to hear their success stories—one never the same as another.

Let me remind you here of the need for both confidentiality and discretion in dealing with high net worth individuals. For that reason, you'll find my stories about my clients general in nature and their names fictitious except in rare instances.

From the standpoint of learning and personal growth, I've found the value of interacting with super successful buyers and sellers of luxury real estate goes beyond measure.

One example involves a man who was among the wealthiest in our small town. Every town has one, and many people may conjure an image of Mr. Potter, the crotchety old businessman in the 1946 movie, *It's a Wonderful Life*.

At the time I was beginning my career, this man—patriarch of a huge family—was referred to as Grandpa John, Uncle John, or simply John. I called him Mr. Smith (not his real name) and knew him to possess both the business acumen of Mr. Potter and the heart of the movie's hero, George Bailey.

I mostly visited Mr. Smith when, in the early days of my career, I felt discouraged and ready to give up my life as a real estate agent. It did, after all, take more than one year for me to sell my first home. And it certainly wasn't in the luxury category by any definition.

Reportedly, Mr. Smith had no more than an eighth-grade education and had worked in land clearing and landscaping. He was so old, he made his first trip to our town in a horse and carriage and grew up experiencing the hardships of the Great Depression firsthand.

During tough economic times, many of his customers couldn't afford to pay him, so they gave him house lots in the subdivisions he worked in.

In part because of this arrangement, he became the largest property owner in town over time. His holdings eventually included scores of houses, hotels, mall properties, and more.

The time I spent talking with Mr. Smith proved to be better than any time I could have spent in an MBA program. He taught me the value of one's word and a handshake; he warned me of the "evils" of overextending with leverage in real estate, and much more.

During my three-plus-decades career, our country has had three major economic downturns, including the current low point starting in 2008. Yet the advice I received from Mr. Smith has stood the test of time.

Among his gems of advice that I've followed:

◈ Don't get cocky.
◈ Don't depend on excessive debt.
◈ Make a plan to pay off your real estate.
◈ Live within your means.

In large part, these constitute the basic reasons my real estate career has survived each of the downturns we've experienced.

In addition to my "schooling" with Mr. Smith, I have had the privilege of interacting with CEOs of Fortune 500 companies as well as other accomplished individuals. Each occasion has been an incredible learning experience.

I have long held the opinion that if executives in major corporations feel confident enough to commit several million dollars to buying a vacation home, their companies might be good ones to invest in. I have rarely gone wrong when I've make my investment decisions this way.

That said, I have NEVER received insider information about any company. The surest way to end a relationship with a corporate executive is to ask for some. On the other hand, my theory is that (with minor yet notable exceptions), if executives have limited confidence in their companies' ability to thrive, they wouldn't be buying second homes in the luxury market.

2

LIFESTYLES OF THE RICH AND FAMOUS

F. Scott Fitzgerald wrote that "the rich are different than you and me." The more you work with high-end individuals, the more you learn that is an absolute understatement.

Here's an example. After a recent showing, I drove a potential buyer back to his own residence. As I pulled into the driveway, I could see exterior painting work in progress: tarps, ladders, and workers sanding and priming the trim preparing it for new paint.

In our conversation, the owner mentioned how he researched the different brands of paint, who manufactures them, and even how they're manufactured. After settling on what he thought was a perfect brand, he got in touch with the CEO of the selected paint company who assigned a factory rep to advise him on the exterior painting of the house. The factory rep actually visited his house, coached the painters, and oversaw the preparation and the application of the new paint, including application thickness, temperature conditions, and humidity during the time the paint would be applied.

This may seem obsessive, but it indicates how wealthy people have precise expectations and high standards—and expect them to be met. They're willing to pay the price and expend the effort to make sure fulfillment of their needs reaches that high standard of quality.

I have separated "clients of means" into four categories: WANNAs, KINDAs, REALLYs, and SUPERs. I admit to being general and perhaps even arbitrary as I came up with these four categories, but they encapsulate the types of personalities I've encountered during my career. Some of the characteristics noted come from an out-of-print book titled *Nine American Lifestyles: Who We Are and Where We're Going* by Arnold Mitchell.

JACK'S FOUR CATEGORIES OF THE WEALTHY

Consider the following descriptions and feel free to develop your own categories—as many as you desire!

WANNAs
Wannas are those people who have reached the point of $1 million in total net worth—that's $1 million after scraping together values on their homes, cars, jewelry, boats, and high-end stainless steel appliances. These folks spend lots of money because appearing wealthy is important to them. They almost always wear nice jewelry; they drive the newest luxury vehicles that are usually leased. They have an idealistic media-driven view of people who are wealthier than they are. They tend to think rich people don't care about price and believe "if you have to ask how much something is, you probably can't afford it." Often heavily in debt, they're highly vulnerable to changes in the economic climate.

Because the beautiful homes in which they reside are heavily leveraged, this group is likely to be a source of short sales and high-end foreclosures.

Often living in wealthy areas and providing services for those in the next three categories, they see all the "fine things" and want them, too. Who can blame them? Beware, though, of their need to play the impossible game of keeping up with the folks in the higher three categories.

What can be discouraging to the WANNAs is reflected in a recent study by the Spectrem Group, a firm that specializes in the study of high net worth individuals (HNWIs). The study noted that only 22% of respondents believe that $1 million makes a person rich.[1]

KINDAs

The next category, the KINDAs, have a net worth greater than $1 million but less than $25 million.

Typically executives, highly skilled professionals, or business owners, they tend to be self-made, trusting individuals who aren't wild about change. This resistance to change especially manifests in their interactions with banks, advisors, and financial institutions. They like dealing with the same people on a long-term basis; they see themselves as unique; they detest being part of a pack. And they love owning things that say "limited edition."

REALLYs

These folks are worth $25 million to $100 million. In most cases, they have made or inherited so much money they have the time and inclination for political activism, most commonly in the form of "getting green." REALLYs are the folks driving hybrid cars.

They tend to be self-absorbed and hate being manipulated or taken advantage of. Usually highly skilled professionals, business owners, or executives, they tend to be well educated. *Most important, they are smart and want everyone to know it.* Typical high-pressure sales techniques are guaranteed to backfire when applied to REALLYs.

SUPERs

Worth $100 million and more, SUPERs may or may not be self-made. They tend to be more politically active than the REALLYs. Usually, a single issue such as political campaigns or, these days, going green consumes much of their free time.

While SUPERs don't necessarily *need* outward signs of wealth or status, they often have them. They might drive a hybrid car to the private airfield where they keep their jet.

CHARACTERISTICS IN COMMON

Certain traits run through of all four categories, plus those in each group possess many of the characteristics of the group below them. At the same time, each can have a difficult time identifying with the group above. This is especially true for the WANNAs who have a naive, media-driven view of the KINDAs.

People in each group tend to think that to be rich, you have to make the grade in the group above. Yet as rich as they may be, they often don't think of themselves as rich. For one thing, they have as much stress as anyone about getting ahead.

Talk to self-made HNWIs and they'll tell a similar story: "I thought that if I could get to one million in net worth, I would have it made. When I arrived at this point, I thought that if I could only build this to five million, I would be all set."

Of course, once that milestone is met, the new level to strive for becomes $10 million. And no doubt people worth $100 million might think having $250 million is needed to be rich.

Texans have a cute way of defining rich. They define a "unit" as $10 million, with the goal of being worth a certain number of "units." Note the use of plural; one unit just does not cut it.

HNWIs in all categories tend to spend like crazy on one or two things and can actually be cheap in other areas. On Cape Cod, for example, the car one owns isn't viewed the same as in other locations of the country. If I were to have my dream real estate car, a Bentley, I would be looked at with suspicion: "What is he trying to prove?" or "Who does he think he is?" In this area, a Realtor® driving a Bentley is perceived as trying too hard. At the same time, in my market, I can spend the equivalent of three Bentleys on a boat and no one would give it a second thought. Boats simply are not perceived as flashy in New England. This relationship could be reversed in your market.

According to the *World Wealth Report for 2009*, a yearly study by Capgemini and Merrill Lynch, "...the recent economic turmoil has taken a heavy toll on high net worth individuals."[2] In fact, according to this same study, at the end of 2008, the world's high net worth population was down 19.9% while their cumulative wealth was down 19.5%.

Put into context, less than 5% of the United States population has a net worth of $1 million or above. When many of these millionaires—especially the WANNAs—are calculating their net worth, they throw everything into the pot: jewelry, homes, cars, artwork, and boats to scrape together their million-dollar net worth.

A stricter definition of a HNWI is used in the *World Wealth Report*[3] and mentioned by Dr. Thomas Stanley in *The Millionaire Next Door*.[4] These authorities define high net worth as $1 million of investable assets excluding primary residence, collectibles, consumables, and consumer durables. Given that definition, less than 1% of the U.S. population could be classified as "millionaires."[5]

As mentioned earlier, another common characteristic running through the four categories is that "people with means" are smart. I don't know why business people in general—and real estate practitioners specifically—think that because people have lots of money, they are carefree and often overpay for what they want—that they are not so smart in that way.

Far from it, given how well they negotiate.

I can assure you that the higher the client is on the net worth scale, the more challenging the sales negotiations are likely to be. SUPERs are tougher negotiators than REALLYs, who are tougher than KINDAs, who are tougher than WANNAs.

If you spend time dealing with SUPERs, you'll quickly conclude that their negotiation skills helped get them to where they are.

CLOTHING AND CARS THE RICH ARE ACCUSTOMED TO

Many agents who contemplate working in the high-price range worry about their clothes, their jewelry, their cars, and the homes they live in. How much do they need to emulate the lifestyle of their wealthy prospects and clients?

Many years of experience have convinced me to never try to match the lifestyles of my high-end clients—good advice for you, too. If you think about the last time you had your house painted and compare it to a wealthy homeowner's approach, you'll realize what I mean.

Nevertheless, it's always within your power to keep up appearances by dressing neatly and professionally. I live in a resort market where people wear shorts and polo shirts in the summer and similar casual but warm clothes in the winter. It has always been my practice to wear jackets, ties, and dress pants no matter what the season is.

Why? I'm not the one on vacation; my clients are. I want to stress the importance of having a high level of professionalism that your attire denotes. Further, I'm here to serve my clients, meet their needs, and exceed their expectations. In this regard, I am not their equal.

And while I shared with you that my ultimate dream real estate sales vehicle would be a Bentley four-door, it's not a practical choice in this market. They do have all-wheel drive, but I can't see myself driving one in a snow storm or down an unpaved road leading to an ocean-side mansion.

All you need is a clean, neat four-door car. As with your car, make sure your office looks professional, neat, and clean. (This is especially true for the restrooms, which should be modern and spotless.)

So never make the mistake of judging others by the cars they drive or the clothes they wear. In my market, people drive Bentleys and Aston Martins; they also drive 30-year-old Ford pickup trucks. Believe it or not, it's not that expensive to lease a Bentley if they choose. And in many cases, fancy clothes, nice cars, and expensive jewelry simply mean the proprietor of these items is deep in debt.

THE KIND OF CAR YOU DRIVE MATTERS

I remember accompanying an agent from my office to a listing appointment for a beautiful seaside residence in a neighboring village. Because it was an estate situation, we knew we'd be meeting with the children of the deceased and their families.

Their forward-thinking parents had purchased the property decades earlier and it had increased in value dramatically. The children and the families who were now the owners of the property did not have the means to maintain the dwelling nor pay the taxes, so they had to sell. Located on one of the most expensive streets in town, this home would fall in the $3 million to $4 million range.

As we pulled up the winding driveway in my real estate vehicle—a four-door high-performance SUV—I noticed the other cars parked there: A Toyota Prius, a Subaru, and a

Hyundai. I was in trouble. My car probably used more gas coming up the driveway than those three cars combined used arriving on Cape Cod from their faraway residences.

Although I made my presentation and a compelling argument for why they should hire our firm to list the property, we did not prevail in the selection process. We had given a price opinion in the mid-$3 million and the heirs listed with another firm that had estimated in the upper $4 million range. I suspect if I were driving a Bentley, they would have thrown me out even before I got to say hello.

This experience provided these additional insights to ponder: First, I actually wondered if I would be forced to get a smaller car or a hybrid for appointments like this, just in case it made a difference. (The trouble is I don't always know until it is too late.) Not only that, I'm likely to run into this type of buyer or seller around town.

Then the perfect solution came to me and has worked like a charm. I keep my bike rack on the back of my SUV. At least I now look green.

Indeed, just this week I was driving to an oceanfront estate down a long, narrow, muddy dirt road. A family of cyclists pulled to the side of the narrow road so I could roll past. Their looks of disapproval at the sight of my SUV interrupting their ride were evident. After I passed, I could see the change in facial expressions in my rearview mirror as they spotted my bike rack.

I don't need to buy a hybrid after all. However, I am careful to never carry my bike on the rack to an appointment. That could signal I had someplace to go afterward and thus lead to questioning if my full attention was on the appointment at hand.

What happened to that property, you may be curious to know? It sold 18 months later for about 5% less than our original suggested price.

I've noticed most well-off individuals have relatives who are less well off than they are. Wealthy individuals tend to take care of others, picking up checks at restaurants, giving loans, buying cars, helping with tuition; inevitably, they're being hit up by somebody for something.

Make sure your attitude of service—being there to serve them and not ask favors—provides a refreshing change from their normal interactions of everybody wanting something from them.

High-End Real Estate Is NOT A Commodity, so You Can't Be a Commodity Either

Challenging the real estate industry today is the public perception that real estate brokers and agents have become a commodity. That implies all practitioners offer the same services: a sign in the yard, an ad in the paper, a listing in the MLS and on various web sites, a pat on the back, and a prayer that the property will sell. Price competition and commission erosion stems from this misperception. The more that real estate agents are perceived as commodities, the more they are forced to compete on price.

Nowhere is it more important to fight the idea of commoditization than in the practice of high-end real estate. You've already learned that high-end buyers and sellers *detest* ordinary, run-of-the-mill *anything*. They crave highly customized service and one-of-a-kind experiences. That's why it's critical to identify and develop Unique Selling Propositions (USPs) with this clientele. Your USPs need to be unique but not just for the sake of being unique; they must bring exceptional value to your clients.

Take a moment to identify the USPs you and your company present to your prospective clients. Perhaps they include your national affiliation, your established, well-known brand, your negotiating skills, your staging expertise, your sphere of influence. Identify as many USPs as you can; without them, you're like every other "me too" agent in the marketplace. Rather, you're a luxury specialist—and your prospects need to recognize you as such.

Just like a doctor consults and diagnoses before he or she prescribes, the luxury specialist follows the same template in all interactions with high-wealth individuals. I suggest moving away from the idea of delivering presentations. Instead, consult, diagnose, and prescribe solutions with confidence. HNWIs know you care about them when you take time to ask questions and qualify them. They want you to understand their wants, needs, desires, and goals. They want you to prescribe solutions with confidence.

How do you gain confidence? Through competence. And how do you gain competence? By applying the principles in this book.

ALWAYS APPLY WIIFM

Once you have achieved the required level of professionalism, you can build strong relationships with the HNWIs in your marketplace. Remember, they do not particularly like change; they want to deal with the same people continually—as long as you can meet their expectations.

Remember WIIFM, the acronym for "what's in it for me." That's what HNWIs care about. It may be fun to talk about your own hobbies and sports, especially when they align with theirs. Trust me, though. They may show interest for a brief polite moment, but never neglect to frame every interaction, every conversation, every statement, and every sentence in WIIFM terms—what's in it for them.

That requires adhering to principles and practices that exude honesty, ethics, and discretion while maintaining their right and expectation to privacy.

Remember this question and ask it often throughout the day: "Is the action I am about to take right now in the best long-term interest of my client(s)?"

FOOTNOTES:
1. Spectrem Group. www.spectrem.com
2. Capgemini/Merrill Lynch *2009 World Wealth Report*. www.us.capgemini.com/worldwealthreport09
3. Ibid.
4. Stanley, Dr. Thomas J. and Danko, Dr. William D. *The Millionaire Next Door*. Pocket Books, a division of Simon & Schuster, 1996. p. 12.
5. Op. cit. Capgemini/Merrill Lynch.

FOUR TRUTHS SET
THE RIGHT MINDSET

TO BEGIN YOUR ODYSSEY INTO THIS BUSINESS, FOUR TRUTHS ARE critical to developing the right mindset for understanding. You may consider some of the four obvious, others counterintuitive. But you'll find they are true with regard to being successful in luxury real estate.

TRUTH #1: IT'S EASIER, BUT NOT NECESSARY, TO
HAVE BEEN BORN RICH AND CONNECTED.
No question. Your success in luxury real estate sales would be easier if you already had money and lots of connections with high-wealth individuals. It also helps if you're a reasonably good athlete on the golf course. Many high-end buyers and sellers put high value on connections, club membership, and even golf handicaps. I can think of many times I did a spectacular listing presentation with PowerPoint, charts, and graphs—including a well-documented Competitive Market Analysis (CMA)—and lost the listing to the seller's golf buddy.

If you have none of these connections or no prowess on the fairways, don't give up. Know that the process just takes longer than it would for "connected" agents. While I do play a little golf now, my skills on the links will never get me a listing or a sale. And even though I play more than ever, I've spent more time on the course as a caddy than a player.

The good news is that while well-connected and wealthy people have a presence in the real estate business, they're not always your strongest competitors. Sure, they tend to be well-schooled, well-networked people from the second and third generations of affluent families. They deem selling real estate a dignified way to make a living once the trust funds have thinned out. And you thought your status was on a par with used car salespeople!

These well-heeled agents are easy to recognize. Those who hope to break into high-end real estate note their demeanor and become discouraged. "I can't get the Thurston Howell elocution down and can't match the connections," they convince themselves.

If that doesn't discourage you, wait until you see the typical business plan of these rich, well-connected agents. Through massive and painstaking research, careful surveillance, and countless interviews, we have pieced together a "day in the life" of one such agent, "Biff." Lead after hot lead comes his way as the day unfolds. Let's follow.

EARLY BREAKFAST
Biff is up earlier than you might imagine, eating a light but satisfying breakfast at the local power breakfast hotspot (likely a corner table at a local restaurant or club). His friends and acquaintances saunter in and out. Some linger only long enough for a quick hello; others stop to refer a friend who wants to buy or sell a mega-property.

LATE BREAKFAST
Biff's second breakfast of the day could be at his Club or at a power breakfast spot where the well-connected wealthy gather or merely pass as ships in the night—dropping another hot lead to Biff on their way to their favorite table.

NINE HOLES OF GOLF
The cool thing about golf is that if you show up mid-morning like Biff does, the starter sets you up with one or three players soon after your arrival. Biff may or may not know these golf companions initially,

but he will by the end of the round. Well before lunch, he has picked up several more hot leads from his new golf buddies who are likely to be Fortune 500 CEOs.

LUNCH AT THE CLUB
In a scene similar to breakfast, people pass by Biff's table to talk with him or his tablemates. Introductions are made. If the new acquaintances don't know that Biff sells high-end real estate, they soon will. Two more easy leads come his way at lunch. After all, they want Biff to like them.

NINE MORE HOLES
After lunch, it's time to head back to the course. Due to all that eating, all that greeting, perhaps even a drink or two—whatever the reason—Biff's mates for the afternoon round will deliver at least one or two hot leads for him before completing the eighteenth hole. I don't know if you are keeping track but I've lost count of the leads. And Biff's day isn't over yet.

By the way, Biff keeps track: he discretely jots a few brief notes in a pocket diary after the visitors leave his presence. Alternatively, he calls the "introducer" later in the day to obtain the details. It's not considered good form to appear to be conducting business at a private club. Pulling out a large diary or laptop would put Biff swiftly out of business.

DRINKS AT THE CLUB
Before heading home, Biff stops by the bar with one or more of his fellow players from the day. Again, more "people of means" come and go, some stopping to say hello, others telling him they know someone who just has to have a large home on the water. Add more hot leads.

EVENING COCKTAILS
Biff heads home for cocktail hour. With his feet up on the comfortable water-view porch, he scans the news in *The Wall Street Journal*. Biff recognizes several names of wheelers and dealers mentioned. He thinks, "Surely I'll run into people who know them and they'll help

with an introduction later in the evening." A long shower, quick snack, and he's off to one of the several cocktail parties on for the evening. On a good night, he'll have several to attend. And, you guessed it, more leads at each event.

By the way, you'll meet female Biffs (I call them Buffys), too. Their typical day is similar; they just skip one or two of the meals and substitute tennis for golf.

Even as I write this, I get depressed. Of course, my description of Biff's day is a bit tongue in cheek. But though it may seem improbable, it's not that far off. I know agents who operate this way, and it creates a successful lifestyle for them.

This form of "prospecting" has never been an option for me—or likely for you, either! Poor golf skills, limited connections, and social skills from a modest background rule out such a typical day for me.

Instead, I focus on how to compete with the Biffs of the world—and share my secrets with you. Perhaps you can guess the main secret: Outwork those for whom real estate sales is an avocation, not a vocation.

TRUTH #2: IT'S ALL IN YOUR HEAD.
Any limitations you perceive as holding you back from being a successful luxury real estate agent are all in your head. Get over the fact that your days won't unfold like those of Biff or Buffy. Having the right mindset as the game changer, there are no exceptions to this truth, especially in high-end real estate.

In fact, having the right mindset may be even more important for success in dealing with high net worth individuals than others. Just like a horse can sense a nervous rider, wealthy people often have honed "BS detectors" and will sense intimidation, insecurity, and insincerity.

The antidote? Be yourself. Be confident and good at what you do.

To out-compete these "born connected" agents as well as other well-established luxury practitioners, be sure to:
- develop a concrete plan to establish yourself as a market expert,
- let the right people know, and

◆ serve them diligently and professionally until they buy, sell, or refer someone who will do one or the other.

The following chapters tell you about how I outworked established agents in the high-end market to gain my share of the action. Was I nervous when I got my first waterfront listing appointment? You bet. Nervous but prepared—like you will be when you apply the principles in this book.

$600 IN SEED MONEY

When I began in 1974, I had only $600 of seed money to start my business—money that actually came from a rear-end collision. My 1967 Ford Maverick (green with black racing stripes down the hood and three-speed shift on the column) got rear-ended in a snowstorm. I didn't fix the car, and with the insurance money I received, I started my business. I even showed property driving around in my damaged Maverick.

I set up my first "office" in the corner of my father's plumbing supply warehouse. Picture my gun-metal gray desk surrounded by stacks of toilet seats. In that space, I even made my own real estate signs. I look back and shake my head. But if I can succeed starting that way, you can succeed, too.

To differentiate myself from the established agents, I consistently produced a 20-plus page narrative appraisal complete with floor plans and comparable adjustments to win a listing. (Chapter 8 on pricing discusses "CMAs by the pound.")

Each evening, I hand-typed 100 personal letters to property owners in my market area. Back then, we had no computers or word processors—not even correction tape. All my letters were individually typed on a Remington fabric ribbon typewriter. To save money, I purchased an old used typewriter that typed in italics rather than a typical font. I guess no one else wanted a machine that created such distinctive pages of text. What an impression these letters must have made!

TRUTH #3: YOU MUST BE PERCEIVED AS AN EXPERT.
It makes sense if you think about it: Wealthy people are used to dealing with experts in all aspects of their lives. Whether they have medical, legal, or tax needs, they have the ability to obtain and therefore expect the best guidance available. Many times, this is a point of honor for them.

In addition, they are used to working with the most experienced practitioners in any field and will accept nothing else. They want to tell their friends that the physician they go to is tops in a particular field, or they hired the same attorney who represented O.J.

Clearly, their circle of experts serve as status symbols, people most certainly worthy of someone like themselves.

This, my friends, provides the golden opportunity for those who want to become luxury real estate agents. Expertise can be acquired, honed, improved, and built upon. You can then use it to provide services that the wealthy will value.

As you will learn in the following chapters, you need to gain expertise in these five critical areas:
    Market and Values (Chapter 4)
    Listing Preparation and Positioning (Chapter 9)
    Pricing (Chapter 8)
    Marketing (Chapters 9 through 20)
    Negotiating (Chapter 22)

TRUTH #4: COMPETENCE AND TRUST LEAD
TO LASTING RELATIONSHIPS.
What's your ultimate goal as a luxury real estate specialist? To become *the* trusted advisor to a group of high-end individuals who call you for your opinion on all real estate matters.

People of means like consistency and discretion. They don't want to share their personal business with countless experts. They do want a small circle of trusted advisors they can turn to as situations arise. Once you achieve this level of expertise and trust, the referrals will come.

Commit this to memory: ***Confidence comes from competence.*** And competence comes through education, practice, and outworking your competition.

4

FOUR ESSENTIAL COMPONENTS
OF PERCEIVED EXPERTISE

As mentioned earlier, wealthy people respect knowledge and those who possess it. This chapter features four components that reveal exactly what knowledge they value and then helps you obtain it. It can also teach you how to let "people of means" in your market know you have the kind of expertise they want.

Component #1: Become a genuine
expert on markets and value.

To become a perceived expert on markets and value in the areas you serve, first target the luxury market in which you want to work. This is easily done by familiarizing yourself with the town or county in which you want to specialize, and identifying the exact areas that have homes in your target value range.

Get your hands on a large-scale map from the appropriate department of your town hall (could be the tax assessor's office or the engineering department). One benefit of using an assessor's map is that it shows individual parcels in the selected area.

Print this map as large as you can, place it on your office wall, and begin to construct a two-year history of your market area.

Pull up all sales history and current offering information in your chosen market. Once you have gathered all this information and placed it graphically on your wall map, then study it, digest it, and internalize it. Indeed, become "one" with it so you're a walking, talking expert on everything that has occurred in your marketplace during the past two years.

On the map, locate all current listings and note their prices, square footage, land area, and how long each one has been on the market. Of course, you can do this on your computer using Google maps or the equivalent, but I think you'll realize a huge benefit in seeing things blown up and taped to the wall in your office.

Plot all the sold properties that feature similar information: land area, dwelling space, and so on. Then for the whole market area of interest, note the days on market, average sales price, average list to sales price ratio, and tax assessment ratios. You'll be able to see this data at a glance.

LOCATION ADJUSTMENT MATRIX
When you are doing price opinions or CMAs in your marketplace, it's imperative that you remain consistent in your assumptions about comparative values throughout the different locations in your area. To do this, create a Location Adjustment Matrix similar to the one shown on the next page.

Here's how to set up a Location Adjustment Matrix. Down the left side of the page, list all the high-end areas in which you plan to specialize. Repeat the locations in the same order across the top of the spreadsheet. You can go to www.jackcotton.com, click on downloads, and get a copy of my location matrix. When you add locations down the left column, they auto fill across the top.

As you study your target markets, you begin to form opinions regarding the comparative value of similar properties in the different locations. For example, you may determine an estate on Egg Island is worth 20% more than a similar estate on North Bay. That's how you keep track of this difference in market value based on locations.

Understand, this is not an exact science. These adjustment percentages are based on your opinion that, in turn, is based on your

Comparable Locations
My Opinion Of Selling Price Differences In Our Market.   As of   Aug-09

Subject Location	East Barnwich Bay View	Little Island	SeaVille	New Caledonia Ocean Front	Location 5	Location 6	Location 7	Location 8	Location 9	Location 10	Location 11	Location 12
East Barnwich Bay View	NA	-30.0%	-30.0%	-15.0%	0.0%	0.0%	0.0%	0.0%	0.0%	0.0%	0.0%	0.0%
Little Island	30.0%	NA	0.0%	0.0%	0.0%	0.0%	0.0%	0.0%	0.0%	0.0%	0.0%	0.0%
SeaVille	30.0%	0.0%	NA	0.0%	0.0%	0.0%	0.0%	0.0%	0.0%	0.0%	0.0%	0.0%
New Caledonia Ocean Front	15.0%	0.0%	0.0%	NA	0.0%	0.0%	0.0%	0.0%	0.0%	0.0%	0.0%	0.0%
Location 5	0.0%	0.0%	0.0%	0.0%	NA	0.0%	0.0%	0.0%	0.0%	0.0%	0.0%	0.0%
Location 6	0.0%	0.0%	0.0%	0.0%	0.0%	NA	0.0%	0.0%	0.0%	0.0%	0.0%	0.0%
Location 7	0.0%	0.0%	0.0%	0.0%	0.0%	0.0%	NA	0.0%	0.0%	0.0%	0.0%	0.0%
Location 8	0.0%	0.0%	0.0%	0.0%	0.0%	0.0%	0.0%	NA	0.0%	0.0%	0.0%	0.0%
Location 9	0.0%	0.0%	0.0%	0.0%	0.0%	0.0%	0.0%	0.0%	NA	0.0%	0.0%	0.0%
Location 10	0.0%	0.0%	0.0%	0.0%	0.0%	0.0%	0.0%	0.0%	0.0%	NA	0.0%	0.0%
Location 11	0.0%	0.0%	0.0%	0.0%	0.0%	0.0%	0.0%	0.0%	0.0%	0.0%	NA	0.0%
Location 12	0.0%	0.0%	0.0%	0.0%	0.0%	0.0%	0.0%	0.0%	0.0%	0.0%	0.0%	NA

study and knowledge of the market. The most important thing is to be consistent. Therefore, you can't say that Egg Island is worth 20% more than a similar estate on North Bay in one CMA, then use 10% in another.

A major benefit of using a Location Matrix is that you are held accountable by the form to be consistent and to give a least a little thought to the reasons for differences in value between and among different locations within your market.

Again, the Location Matrix I use clearly states it is my opinion as of a specified date.

ASSESSMENT RATIOS

Some agents as well as consumers have difficulty conceptualizing assessment ratios. Let me explain. This number is determined by dividing the sales price by the current property tax assessment. If a property sold for $1,100,000 and the current tax assessment was $1,000,000, the assessment ratio indicates this property sold for 110% of its assessed evaluation. Make a point of calculating this figure for each of the sales in your target area and then be aware of the average ratios for your selected market area. Enter your results on the map you pinned to the wall in your office.

Assessment ratios assist you in making general statements about your market, although a correlation between the assessment and selling price for a specific property is not always present. Rather, these ratios are best suited to making statements such as "homes on the eastern shore of Mytown typically sell for one-hundred-five percent of assessment."

It's possible that some sales have occurred at 85% of assessment number and others at 115%. The value in knowing the average is that when a seller holds out for an offering price that's 145% of selling price, you have the ammunition to respond in a researched, quantitative manner.

For example, you would say, "Mr. and Mrs. Seller, properties similar to yours have sold this year at an average of 90% of tax assessment. The offer we have now is 105% of assessment, which represents a great price for you in this market." It is more effective to be able to use market statistics in presenting an offer rather than saying, "This is a great offer; you should take it!"

BUILDING COSTS

It is good for you to know the costs to build luxury homes in your market for several reasons. First and foremost, people are going to ask you.

Secondly, construction costs in any market and especially the one we're in today, set the upper limit of value for a home. It makes sense that only in rare cases is a buyer going to pay more for a property than it would cost to rebuild.

Keep three questions in mind when determining building costs:
- What is the cost to build a home in your market area?
- What are homes selling for per square foot?
- What is the absorption rate, calculated by the number of homes listed for sale in a certain area divided by the number of homes sold there in the past 12 months?

Interview the top custom builders in your market to get an idea of construction costs. Most custom builders are reluctant to give cost figures on a square-foot basis, but most will give a range. Because of the high-end features and large spaces in luxury homes, generalizing costs is extremely difficult for them.

In many respects, luxury home construction is not unlike commercial construction. Larger, more sophisticated heating systems, hot water delivery systems, and electrical requirements usually go beyond those in typical homes.

We have witnessed companies accustomed to building regular homes grab the opportunity to make lots of money building large luxury homes—with disastrous results. Why? There's a huge difference in scale. You can't run the same half-inch water supply line to a bath at the end of a 16,000 square-foot home that you would use in a 2,000 square-foot ranch-style home. The owners will not be happy when they turn on a faucet in the master bath to be greeted with a trickle of water, even with the tap fully open.

ABSORPTION RATES

Absorption rates are calculated by ascertaining the number of properties actively listed for sale and dividing by the number of sales that occurred during a given time, usually the last 12 months. (It's helpful to create price adjustment spreadsheets that can calculate rates automatically from the data entered.)

Let's say 42 homes between $1.5 million and $2 million are currently for sale in a given area of your market. During the past 12 months, seven homes have sold, making the absorption rate seven each year. This tells you there's a six-year supply of homes in your market in this price bracket (42 homes/7 sales per year = 6 years).

This information is valuable to convey to the potential seller in this neighborhood who wants to price his or her home above your recommendation. If there is a six-year supply of homes, and you actually want yours to sell in a timely fashion, you need to be priced below the prevailing level of current inventory. Remember, many high-end sellers are business people who will relate to the logic of data like this, so it's important to communicate in these terms.

For example, in a high-end golf course development in my area, 27 properties are currently for sale. Homes in this neighborhood start at about $1 million and max out at around $3 million. In the last 12 months, only three transactions have taken place in this area. Using an absorption rate calculation, we conclude there's a nine-year supply of homes in this development (27 homes/3 sales per year = 9 years). This is a prime piece of information you need when providing value opinions to owners of (or people connected to) properties in this location.

Again, I would explain to the prospective seller when a home goes on the market in any price range, the laws of economics dictate that the order in which the homes offered for sale find buyers will be dictated by the price and condition of the competing offerings. That is to say, the better the price and condition, the more likely a particular property is to sell before the others.

The beauty of a seller's market—one with limited inventory—is that buyers often have to settle for what is available. It only makes sense that if there is an over-supply as indicated by an absorption rate of nine years, you need to price to the market if you expect a sale in the near term.

STUDY YOUR COMPETITION

To better understand dynamics in your market, I suggest doing a SWOT (Strengths, Weaknesses, Opportunities, Threats) analysis. This requires that you list the agents who are going to be your competition in your chosen market and study their modus operandi in all four areas that make up SWOT.

Strengths: What are these agents good at and where do they excel? Are they predominantly listing or selling agents? Perhaps one agent gets most of the listings but there's no clear leader among those who bring buyers.

Why are they good at what they do? Are they hobbyists like Biff or Buffy, or are they working a carefully designed plan? Are their listings priced close to current market value, or do they hold them for months and subject their sellers to numerous price reductions? What commission rates are they charging?

Weaknesses: In which areas are they not performing as well as they could be? Perhaps their companies are in an upheaval or maybe they negotiate deals poorly. Are they agents who take listings at any price or at a reduced fee?

Opportunities: Despite initial appearances, opportunities can be found. If they simply don't exist, you'd better find another market to specialize in!

SNIFFING OUT OPPORTUNITIES

I think rampant commission cutting in a market can present a great opportunity for agents. Here's an example. A while ago, we opened an office in a high-end market in which the leading agents were cutting fees by one or two points at the time of listing. This tells me they're perceived as commodities in their market; they believe they have nothing of value to offer sellers over their competitors. To compete, their mindset says they have to cut fees.

If you can present a value proposition with meaningful, valuable points of difference, you can make inroads faster than you might in another market. Applying this approach, our new office became number two in its targeted market in its first full year of operation.

Threats: Where are the speed bumps and roadblocks that could impede your success in your target high-end market? Has an existing company just acquired a luxury affiliation that will give it an edge in the market? What other threats could derail your plans?

COMPONENT #2: WRITERS ARE PERCEIVED AS EXPERTS.
As you read this, you likely assume that your writing expertise should center on high-end real estate. Quite by accident, however, I learned that writers can be perceived as experts no matter what topic they write about! If you are sending letters to the editor, writing and placing advertorials in your local newspaper, or producing and sending reports directly to trusted advisors or high net worth individuals, over time, you'll be regarded as an expert. Remember, "people of wealth" deal only with experts, no matter what the field.

Your ultimate goal in reaching out through your writing is to reinforce your prospective clients' perception of you as an expert on value and real estate in your area.

MY ACCIDENTAL AUTHORSHIP SUCCESS

I can back up this statement with a story from my life. Several years ago, our beloved family dog passed away. As a way to memorialize his relationship with me and with my children, I crafted a small "book" called A Dog's Guide to Life: Lessons From Moose. *I printed the pages from my computer using scanned photographs of Moose with my two children. The pages were bound on the machine we keep in the office for binding high-end listing presentations.*

Unknown to me, agents in my office secured a copy and, at Christmas, presented me with a dozen or so spiral-bound Kinko's copies to give to friends and family. After that, a Kinko's-bound book fell into the hands of a friend who had written several books of her own. She passed it on to her publisher who immediately liked it and published A Dog's Guide to Life. *The book—now in its second printing—has nothing to do with real estate but a lot to do with the business of life.*

I can't even tell you how many times this book has brought both buyers and sellers to me.

In one instance, a seller called me solely because he was touched by this book. She listed a $7 million property with me and it ultimately sold for more than $10 million. Imagine if I had actually written a book on real estate!

WAYS TO BUILD YOUR WRITING EXPERTISE

Writing can be one of the most intimidating aspects of marketing because many folks don't consider themselves good writers. If you feel that way, I suggest enrolling in an online writing class or signing up for classes at your local community college. Alternatively, you can contract with a ghostwriting service or dictate your thoughts into a recorder or have a writer interview you while running a recorder. You can then turn to services such as www.ewordsolutions.com to transcribe your recording into text. Make the corrections and additions you want, and your writing is done.

START WITH A COMPELLING HEADLINE

As a writer, I've found that once a captivating headline is written, the rest of the content seems to flow—especially when the topic highly interests you.

For instance, whenever I'd stand in the checkout line at the supermarket, I'd always glance at the magazine rack waiting for my turn to feed the conveyer belt and cash register. Invariably, my eye was drawn to *Cosmopolitan* magazine (and others of its kind). Reading the headlines, I realized they almost always began with either a number or an imperative verb. Knowing that the publishers of these magazines spend millions of dollars to understand what attracts customers to purchase their magazine, I paid attention!

I have also noticed that the most common numbers used in a headline are 7, 10, 12, and 21. My all-time favorite number is 7—7 seas, 7 deadly sins, 7 dwarfs, 7 habits of highly successful people...you get the idea.

I suggest you picture the eye-catching headlines splashed on the cover of mass market magazines and convert them to headlines that would hold the interest of a high net worth potential home seller. Instead of "21 Celeb Secrets That Work on Everyone," how about "21 Value-Enhancing Secrets That Work to Sell Every Luxury Home"? Or, change "10 Things Guys Notice Instantly" to "10 Things Luxury Home Buyers Notice Instantly."

Once you have created your compelling headline, you have essentially promised your readers details that must be fulfilled in the body of your report.

GLEAN INFORMATION FROM THOSE AROUND YOU

If you are having trouble gathering information, drop by your local town hall and talk to the tax assessor about his or her perception of property values in your area. You might ask questions like these:

- How many property abatement applications does the office receive in the normal course of the year?
- What are the most outlandish reasons people cite in requesting an abatement?
- What do you find are the most effective arguments people make when trying to get their property tax assessment lowered?

The information obtained from these interviews will help you construct a report, article, or advertorial that may well be read and remembered by high net worth individuals and their advisors.

HOW TO WRITE ARTICLES

Let me suggest the following approach I use when writing articles.

- ◈ ***Start with an outline***. Our bodies are built on a skeleton; so is a well-written article. The outline you start with becomes the skeleton of your work.
- ◈ ***Move on to an introductory paragraph***. This puts forth your topic and refers to no more than three main points. Ask, "What does the reader learn or gain from reading this work?" Then write your answer in the first paragraph.
- ◈ ***Discuss each main point in the paragraphs that follow***. For a short piece, you might write one paragraph per point. When you finish one point, start a new paragraph.
- ◈ ***Summarize with a final paragraph***. Pull your main points together and consider ending with a "call to action." Ask, "What should the reader do to take action on the points you have presented?" Then write your answer in the concluding paragraph.

WRITE "LETTERS TO THE EDITOR"

Don't overlook writing letters to the editor of print media you know wealthy people read. The easiest ones to get noticed in, of course, are your local newspapers. Keep in mind that many high net worth individuals subscribe to the local paper so they can keep in the loop, even if they're not full-time residents. Writing advertorials (an article that costs money to place) or letters to the editor (that don't cost money but may not be selected for print) can be effective in getting their attention.

I once wrote a letter to the editor of the local newspaper about conservation issues that were affecting waterfront property owners. I heard minor comments about my letter in the days that followed, but about five or six months later, I got a request for an appointment to list a $5-plus million waterfront property. *This was based solely on the owner reading my letter and feeling like he had connected with me.*

When deciding where to send your articles, advertorials, or letters to the editor, it's important to know where buyers who have recently purchased in your area come from. Again, looking at my local Cape Cod market, I know that upward of 85% of all high-end buyers come from within a 45-mile radius of Boston. I also know that 75% of them come from the financial industry. From an age standpoint, most are in their mid to upper 50s. These demographics give me clues about what subjects they might read.

If your local paper won't print your letter, send it out as a newsletter to your market area.

Tap into the Power of Written Communication
I learned from a wonderful teacher during my high school years the importance, mechanics, and joy of writing. While there's always room for improvement, this skill has been an integral part of my building a successful business during the past three decades. Never underestimate the importance and power of written communication.

Keep these principles in mind when you write:

- *Believe that writing still matters.* In this world of short attention spans conditioned by 10-second sound bites, channel surfing, texting, and staccato e-mails, the art of writing is becoming lost. Still, people of means respect writers and give them a place of authority in their minds.
- *Make sure a good writing reputation is well-deserved.* That requires practice. Writing each day is like exercising. You'll find that even writing five thank you notes a day will stretch your creativity. And imagine the difference in the 1,300 lives of those who receive them every year!
- *Understand that you have a message.* No one sees the world as you do. Your perspective on events, principles, and stories is unique and important. Share it in writing.
- *Believe that people care about your message.* Careful and thoughtful expression of your ideas will greatly interest readers (and potential clients) once you "welcome them in" to your sphere through your writing.
- *How you present your writing matters.* If you want someone else to take the time to read what you have written, make a positive impression. People do judge books by their covers. That means proper grammar, spelling, and punctuation are critical. Neat formatting, clean paper, and a dignified cover

letter go a long way toward packaging your writing in a way that's congruent with the quality of your content. This applies to EVERYTHING you write—from letters, brochures, web site, and ad copy to reports and eventually the books you'll write!

COMPONENT #3: SPEAKERS ARE PERCEIVED AS EXPERTS.

When I tell agents they need to go on the local speaking circuit to talk about real estate, markets, and value, most of them look like a deer caught in headlights. After all, speaking in public is feared more than death itself. As comedian Jerry Seinfeld once said, that means most people at funerals would rather be in the casket than delivering the eulogy.

I'm petrified every time I speak in front of an audience. You, too? I've learned that it's important to find a way to overcome it and get the job done. Why? Because people who speak on topics of real estate, value, and markets are perceived as experts. In fact, public speaking is among the fastest ways to become recognized and valued as an expert in your area.

TIPS FOR CREATING SPEECHES

- **Borrow titles from articles**. Turn the headlines for articles you've written into titles or topics for speeches.
- **Use PowerPoint slides sparingly**. They convey important information in graphic ways, but don't let them become a crutch.
- **Don't put too much information on a slide**. Each slide should include only a few bullet points, images, charts, or graphs. The simpler the better.
- **Avoid reading points or paragraphs from your slides**. Your speech should be in your head and spoken with confidence, not read from your PowerPoint slides.

Once you have written your speech, practice by delivering it to a friendly audience, perhaps your fellow agents at an office meeting. I wrote a talk called "7 Fundamentals of Cape Cod Real Estate" and tested it on the agents in our company. Because of their comments,

I made changes and enhancements, then I went "live" in front of different organizations in the marketplace.

BOOKING SPEECHES

Countless people in your community book interesting speakers for their clubs, organizations, or events. If you think speaking in public is difficult, try being the person in charge of finding (for free) speakers whose talks are interesting, informative, timely, and topical—and who don't put attendees to sleep.

Many business organizations or Chambers of Commerce have weekly or monthly meetings and always need speakers. Seek Rotary Clubs and other service clubs.

When I gave a talk about the Cape Cod real estate market to members of a local club, it was well received. But here's what astounded me. Several days later while attending a function sponsored by a similar organization, several people told me they'd heard how informative my talk was. They were sorry that were unable to make it. You can get almost as much mileage from the people who didn't hear your speech as from those who did!

The very fact that you advertised, promoted, and delivered a talk cements the idea that you are an expert in local real estate. And that, my friend, should be your goal: Differentiating yourself as an expert in and on the market—even in the minds of people who don't hear you speak!

COMPONENT #4: ENDORSED AGENTS ARE PERCEIVED AS EXPERTS.

As you successfully apply Components #1, #2, and #3, always ask for letters of endorsement from those you have served. These letters carry the most perceived value if they come from an attorney, CPA, trust officer of a bank, or person booking speakers for local organizations. Make these endorsements and references part of your curriculum vitae and promotion package.

Again, high net worth individuals value expertise. You can connect with them by gaining that expertise in your specific market area. Emphasize your qualifications and your knowledge about the marketplace, but don't necessarily stress your personal production.

For example, do you think that a high net worth homeowner is going to respond more to "I was the number one agent in my company, market, or state last year" or to "My skills in negotiation and positioning of listings for sale result in sales prices that average ninety-four percent of list price rather than the market average of eighty-nine percent."

In every field, writers and speakers are perceived as experts. Once you have articles and speeches under your belt, endorsements and references naturally follow.

Pursue these ways of making your expertise known and wealthy clients will pursue you.

5

THE EXPERTISE
HNWI'S CRAVE

Now you have this information, background, knowledge, and value expertise, how do you let high net worth individuals (HNWI) know you're ready to be of service?

You've heard the saying, "The way to a man's heart is through his stomach." Well, the way to an HNWI's heart is through his or her wallet. Specifically, if you can provide the market information the attorney or tax professional will use to help shield their wallet from the taxman, you have the best "in."

From experience, I can tell you that "people of means" are obsessed with taxes—all taxes. Their minds constantly roil with thoughts of income taxes, estate taxes, sales taxes, and most relevantly, property taxes.

I am sure my market is like yours in that homeowners pay vast sums of money in property taxes. In our area on Cape Cod, people can pay more than $100,000 a year in taxes on homes they may use for six to eight weeks during the year. Indeed, some homes require $500,000 in yearly taxes.

If this isn't bad enough, after the town collects all this money from people who use few of the municipal services offered, it gives them all kinds of grief if they want to add to their dwelling, construct a pier, or improve their view of the water. The wealthy often feel abused by this practice. If you attend social gatherings, discussions almost always turn to their issues with property value and taxes.

In addition to property taxes, consider the angst among HNWIs caused by estate taxes. Depending on one's state of residence, taxes due at death can be enormous. Imagine having a million-dollar estate tax due on a vacation residence upon the death of a family member. You can see why the wealthy are concerned and why having an estate plan in place to minimize this tax liability is critical.

This is where you come in. Obsession with taxes—both property and estate—lead to obsession with property values. Consider the following e-mail that arrived in my inbox. It's typical of many I receive throughout the year. (Note: Private information was removed and the names were changed.)

From: dwlistem@msn.com
Sent: Wednesday, December 02, 2009 11:04 am
To: Cotton, Jack
Subject: home assessment

Hi Jack,

Hope all is well with you despite the grip of a somewhat lethargic real estate market. We all hope things will begin to look brighter within the next year.

In the meantime Happy and I have wondered whether our home at 123 Big House Way, Clamville is on target with comparable homes from an assessment standpoint. I'm told that you may be the guru to answer that question! Could you get in touch with me so that we could discuss how we/ you could go about determining that and what it would entail?

A phone call might be the best way to discuss. We are at xxx-xxx-xxxx.

Thanks—look forward to hearing from you.

Dewey Listem

Like this wealthy real estate owner, most need yearly updates citing the fair market value of their holdings. They're constantly updating their estate plans and looking for ways to reduce or eliminate taxes. What's my point? Become one of the cadre of experts HNWIs rely on. It's wise to get to know others in this cadre and find out how to connect with them. Among them are CPAs, attorneys, bank trust officers, and financial planners.

1. CPAs

HNWIs regularly turn to certified public accountants or CPAs. I suggest you send letters and make phone calls to CPAs in your area to make them aware of your market expertise. Include a sample CMA or value opinion letter, blacking out any private information.

2. ATTORNEYS

HNWIs rely on attorneys for issues such as estate planning and dissolution, asset protection, and tax planning and reduction.

Again, sending a simple letter and making frequent contacts to attorneys in your area will result in future business. Especially connect with those who specialize in real estate, trusts, and estates.

3. BANK TRUST OFFICERS

Often, wealthy people have arrangements with banks to become the trustees of their estates once they pass on. During the course of time, these trust officers need updates of the fair market value of real estate that is either held in trust or would be held in trust at a given point in time. At the time the client does pass away, another valuation is needed. Again, marketing your services to these individuals is critical.

Research the banks not only in your area but in major cities outside of your area in places where HNWIs have primary or secondary residences.

4. FINANCIAL PLANNERS

Financial planners also need to know that you are a competent source of market information. They certainly need to know you're in a position to provide expert advice on current market value of specific properties at any time. An important part of their job requires them to update files of the wealthy clients with current market value information. As values change, the estate plan and the advice offered by the financial planner will also change. If he or she is not aware of market changes, ineffective financial plans can result. You can make their jobs easier. Once these professionals have a relationship with you based on a timely production of value opinions, the potential for referrals expands enormously.

Think about this: To whom will they show enduring gratitude when it's pointed out that financial plans are based on inaccurate market values of luxury real estate assets so they can be corrected? That's right, you the expert. And who will they think of when it's time to sell that asset? Correct again.

CONNECT WITH TAX PAYERS DIRECTLY
A great time to contact high net worth property owners is three or four months before your town is set to release new tax assessments. Different towns have various schedules for reassessing property. Massachusetts, for instance, requires evaluations to be updated no less than every three years while some towns update their values every year. That gives you numerous opportunities to provide updated market opinions to luxury real estate owners.

Many owners of high-end real estate own their real estate in various types of trusts. The type of ownership or trust is immaterial; what's important is that updates of fair market value of properties held in these trusts are needed every tax year. Remind owners of expensive property well before the April 15 tax deadline that you have the expertise to provide these opinions of value.

CONSTRUCT A TAX EVENT CALENDAR
How do you make the move from being an expert to a trusted advisor? By constantly reminding clients and prospective clients of their need for marketplace updates.

Once your services to conduct independent valuations for either HNWIs or their current trusted advisors have been retained, then use your database or tickler system to remind them of the need for an update every year.

I believe you'll find that when someone decides to sell a luxury property, the name on the bottom of a valuation letter that has crossed the desk of either the property owner or another one of their trusted advisors will likely be the one called in to list and sell the property. Make sure that name is yours.

6

CULTIVATING HIGH
NET WORTH CLIENTS

YES, THE REAL ESTATE INDUSTRY IS A RELATIONSHIP-BASED BUSI-
ness. This is never truer than in the luxury end of the market. High net
worth individuals like to "hang" with others who are like themselves;
they want to deal with people they know or are known by someone
they know. It's really that simple.

Traditionally, agents have been focused on "farming" geographic
territories to build their agencies. Typical real estate farming techniques—using recipe cards, pumpkins, and magnetic calendars delivered to neighborhoods—are simply not effective in high-end markets.
Depending on the person you listen to, real estate trainers, speakers,
and practitioners make the case that the concept of "farming" in real
estate is dead; it's for the losers in the business.

Remember, your goal is to be perceived as an expert, especially
when it comes to luxury real estate values in your market. However,
having and sharing the best recipe for oatmeal cookies or the schedule of the local sports team is not the type of expertise you want to
be known for.

I disagree with the opinion that "farming is for losers" in the real
estate business. At the same time, while I have the deepest respect
and admiration for those in the farming industry, to me, the term

"farming" connotes hot dusty work on a noisy tractor with the pungent smell of manure hanging in the air. It has appeal to me as a hobby, but not my vocation.

That said, if you're not a three-handicap golfer born into a wealthy and well-connected family, cultivating clients can present a challenge and you need a way to do it. Therefore, how can not-yet-connected agents prospect for high-end clients buying and selling properties without the mundane efforts of "farming"?

The answer? Instead of "farming," think "gardening."

Gardening is farming at a more sophisticated level. "Weed this patch over here, feed the roses near it, and cut back the hydrangeas over there."

Two kinds of gardening allow you to take a direct approach in prospecting for clients—"geographic gardening" and "people gardening."

Applying the principles of geographic gardening, an agent selects a defined geographic area in which he or she wants to dominate the market and becomes an expert by studying it well (as described in Chapter 4). Reaching out based on an organized plan of action can yield results for two main reasons: (1) wealthy people like to be around people who are like themselves, and (2) your goal is to make their spheres your sphere. Let's examine them.

BE AROUND LIKE-MINDED PEOPLE

Properties in our area of Cape Cod tend to be more expensive than other parts of the Cape because it's tucked away off of the main roads with lots of interconnecting waterways. It's rare for a buyer to "drop in" and look for real estate here without some sort of connection. In 99% of the cases, a people connection—a friend, relative, or associate—provides the draw.

"Geographic gardening," therefore, can yield results as high net worth individuals (HNWIs) are given the opportunity to "hand pick" their neighbors. Often, a sale occurs when a neighbor purchases adjacent property for added privacy or to keep for a family member.

Implementing a system of value-added mailings sent to a geographic garden can produce results over time. Consider the following list of sample topics from which to seed your gardening plot. Be sure to include a market update with every contact—information they value highly as noted in Chapter 5.

- ◆ Previous year-in-review
- ◆ Prognostications for the new year
- ◆ Interpretations of economic news and their affect on your garden
- ◆ Tax assessment data and updates
- ◆ Offers from market affiliates (See Chapter 10)
- ◆ Exceptional sales and listings
- ◆ Press clips in which you are featured
- ◆ Newsletter
- ◆ Magazine (yours or your company's)
- ◆ Property tax update
- ◆ Local ordinance issues such as changes to Board of Health or Conservation Regulations.

At one time or another, our agency has used all of these ideas to add value to property owners in our "garden." Currently, our full-color magazine, *Cape Cod Style*, has been the focus of our gardening. Sending out newsletters with market wrap-ups and statistics has also been successful in keeping our firm "top of mind" with owners of luxury real estate in our market.

And remember, because luxury property owners are obsessed with their taxes, any information you can send in this area provides tremendous value.

MAKING *THEIR* SPHERES *YOUR* SPHERE

"People gardening" targets groups of people already known to the agent (even to a minor extent) regardless of where they live. With this concept, *you* have a sphere, *they* have a sphere, and you want to make *their* spheres *your* sphere. (Chapter 18 addresses the value of gardening your sphere of influence, or SOI, in greater length.)

"People gardening" works because the decision to buy or sell high-end real estate is often impulsive. Remember the man who decided to sell his home after the dumpster noise in his new neighborhood bothered him? Similarly, a high-end owner of real estate will wake up in the morning, look out the window, and wonder what the view of the bay would look like from a different angle or location on the same body of water. The exact afternoon the call goes out, the house goes on the market, and the search begins for a home that's sometimes only half a mile away.

I expect it also happens that a high net worth property owner wakes up in the morning and can't think of any more projects to oversee at his or her property: pools and tennis courts have been redone, the kitchen has been remodeled, and so on.

New projects often keep many people active, feeling useful, and even entertained. The decision to put a home on the market and buy another in need of updating and renovation can be made within an hour. So the existing property goes on the market and the search for a new challenge begins.

This practice of musical houses is why it's critical to be "top of mind" with high net worth owners of real estate in your area.

Here are suggested ways you can become part of their spheres so you *are* top of mind when a decision to buy or sell gets made.

Mailings: The prospect of doing regular mailings, whether in the form of newsletters or just postcards, intimidates many agents. Even the beginning agent on a small budget can subscribe to services that provide these customizable materials at reasonable cost. They can be tweaked and personalized with local information and commentary with minimal time investment.

To be successful, mailings should be consistent, planned about a year in advance, and reflect the quality of the service and product you represent. The services, of course, are you; the product is the high-end real estate you represent.

As I mentioned at the beginning of this chapter, recipe cards, sports schedules, and other similar packaged mailing systems can be effective agent marketing pieces in normal markets. Ask this question before settling on any mailer or other piece of marketing: Will this postcard, flyer, newsletter or ad serve the purpose of cementing my image as an expert in luxury real estate? You can see why recipe cards don't cut it in the high end.

Sending out high-quality aerial photographs of the area taken at different times of the year has worked well for us in the past. And most popular have been postcard reproductions of the work of local artists. In that one-and-a-half-second span when a recipient decides to keep or trash a piece of mail, an aerial photo or reproduction of a painting featuring a recognizable scene in your marketplace almost always "makes the cut" and survives the flight to the trash can. Often the photographs are perceived as too valuable and they stay around. People love aerial photos because, unlike maps, they can see their own property as well as its surroundings.

One year during a particularly harsh winter, we took several aerial photos of the ocean, which was actually frozen solid. The photos highlighted salt water inlet bays with massive windblown snow and tide-driven ice along the shoreline. We sent them out the following summer, which was an unusually warm one. They made quite an impression as the talk of the party circuit during the summer season. Most seasonal residents don't think much about their property in the off season, but during a stretch of 90-degree July weather, they got a charge out of seeing their second-home surroundings looking like Antarctica.

Doing the reverse can also be effective—sending beautiful aerial pictures of the area during the height of the season to residents while they're living in cold-weather areas.

If you visit art galleries in your area, you can often arrange to purchase a painting along with the reproduction rights for a given number of postcard mailings. Not only is it possible that the painting will be a nice addition to your office or residence, but these kinds of mailings are unusual, topical, and often retained. You might even consider, after seeking professional tax advice, making the artwork purchase a business expense!

For mailings to have a classy appearance, always use first-class mail. That takes the form of using a hand-applied postage stamp whenever possible.

INNOVATIVE, IMPRESSIVE, EXPENSIVE

One time over a decade ago, we created what I'm sure at the time was the first hardcover brochure for a single estate in our area. It was a huge undertaking that started with hours of photography, layout, and art direction. We then had to find a company that could bind the book and deliver a quantity of 1,000. The cover had a die cast indentation into which a color photograph of the residence was applied. This impressive piece was hugely expensive to produce.

One thing we had not considered was the cost to mail the 1,000 books once they arrived. In fact, that expense of $5 to $6 in postage per piece would have put the project over the top.

But this setback gave us the idea of hand delivering them. We found two college students, dressed them in their Sunday best, and sent them off in our agency's car to deliver the hardcover books to high net worth property owners in the area. Each recipient was asked to "sign for a special delivery from Cotton Real Estate." Voila! We accomplished our distribution at a fraction of the cost and made a bigger impression in the long run. Needless to say, we were the talk of the town for the marketing piece, the likes of which no one had seen before, as well as for our unique form of delivery.

Calling: I have experimented over the years with direct mail, cold calls, and combinations of the two. Anyone will tell you that the percentage return on either of these activities alone is miniscule. What returned the greatest results was to call first with a brief explanation of a mailing they were about to receive. I simply asked them to keep an eye out for it. Most all agreed to do so, and the response garnered from calling before mailing surpassed that of calling after mailing or doing either one on its own.

Gardeners know that a successful "crop" comes from making a plan and executing it consistently over time. A master gardener would never till, plant, water, and feed and then expect a beautiful floral display by the weekend. Similarly, the luxury agent needs to make a plan and execute it over time. Results come gradually, just like they would for a master gardener. Unlike the night before a final exam at college, you can't "cram" gardening into luxury real estate and expect to succeed.

7

THE LISTING APPOINTMENT
TWO-STEP

IF YOU HAVE FOLLOWED MY ADVICE SO FAR, SOONER THAN LATER
the opportunity to present yourself at a listing appointment will arise.
You're meeting face to face with people who could potentially trust
you to steer their most expensive asset to a successful sale.

How do you prepare for that encounter? What should you know
and teach your new clients during the preliminary and follow-up
appointments? Understanding the importance of preparing ahead
of time and having your ducks in a row provides an ounce of preven-
tion that you'll find is worth a pound of cure, especially in the world
of luxury real estate.

PRESENT A PROFESSIONAL PRELISTING PACKAGE

I have always subscribed to a three-part, two-appointment listing
process. For me, the prelisting package is the underpinning of pro-
ductive listing appointments. It serves these two purposes:

(1) it makes you accountable, and

(2) it outlines the whole process.

When it comes to accountability, if you're on your own, it's easy
to let something slide. However, if you present a carefully planned
and crafted prelisting package to a potential seller *before* your first

appointment and you don't meet the standards it sets, well, best to pack it in. You're wasting your time and the client's. But having built-in accountability demands you meet your own expectations and deliver that million-dollar service to your sellers. The professionalism of your prelisting package sets up that expectation.

In terms of outlining the whole process, your package summarizes your company, its strengths, talents, and successes. It should consist of a high-quality folder with a photo of you and/or your company's logo. It includes your résumé, samples of marketing materials, and succinct bullet points describing your expertise, experience, and results.

Before showing up for the first appointment, it's impressive to deliver your prelisting package by overnight service or local courier. You could also set up a pact with another agent in your office: You deliver mine; I'll deliver yours!

I include a detailed page-by-page description of my prelisting book, which you'll find in Appendix B. You may use it as a template to create your own or take ideas from it to enhance your current one.

THE FIRST APPOINTMENT

At your first appointment—and those that follow—your aim is to make your potential clients feel comfortable, like they already know you before you meet.

Use the first appointment as an information-gathering session. Also, it is an additional opportunity to differentiate yourself from the competition. This begins with your car, your dress, your demeanor, and your actions. As mentioned in Chapter 2, your car doesn't have to be a Rolls Royce or Bentley, but it should be clean with no visible dirt, duct tape, or body damage.

Dress professionally. I suggest a jacket and tie for gentlemen and appropriate business attire for ladies. Arrive on time, always carry a briefcase or portfolio with a blank pad, and have a pen at the ready. I cannot tell you how many times I have accompanied agents on listing appointments, only to discover they came empty-handed. A big no-no.

I don't care what you're writing when the potential seller is talking; you need to be writing. The seller has to feel that everything he or she says is held in highest regard by you. In reality, their words *should* be extremely important to you.

Because many homes are large and detailed, I typically walk the property first with the seller for a quick overview. Once we're finished, I go through the house again more slowly taking careful notes and room-by-room measurements. I always assume I'll get the listing, so I take time to note the details of the property, dictating room-by-room descriptions into a handheld digital tape recorder.

I know that most of my competitors don't do this. At the same time, I also know that when I present my price opinion at a subsequent appointment, the seller will remember the care and diligence I took in my first appointment. (Note: I use a web provider called eWordSolutions.com to transcribe all my room-by-room dictation. This service is fast, reasonable, accurate, and wonderful to deal with.)

To get ready for the appointment, I will have researched and copied the plans, deeds, restrictions, assessments, and easements—everything I can find about the property that might affect value and marketability. If the seller mentions something about a lot line or boundary issue during our first meeting, it's impressive to pull a related plan from the file. Many times the seller will not have received one by the time of the appointment.

The first appointment is also the best time to discuss local laws of agency—another way of differentiating yourself from your competitors. Consider using a PowerPoint presentation to communicate this important topic. Just because you're with high net worth individuals, you'd be surprised how infrequently some buy real estate and how little they actually know about the business of agency.

Because agency laws and practice vary across the country, you will be discussing the specifics in your area.

It doesn't matter if you work as a seller's agent, designated agent, facilitator, or disclosed dual agent. What matters is the client knows what type of agency you and your company practice and what to expect.

As in any price range, determining the seller's motivation is critical. The seller doesn't always *need* to sell, but many times the *desire* to sell can be strong enough to give the seller a degree of motivation. This motivation tends to be inversely proportional to the number of times you're told the family doesn't need to sell, especially in this tight market.

Sometime before the end of the first appointment, the seller always asks my impression of what the asking price should be. I resist the temptation to give away my thoughts on price at this point. On the rare occasions when I've broken this rule, I've almost always regretted it. By adhering to the pricing process explained in Chapter 8, I dramatically increase the chances of my "getting it right."

I tell sellers that once I have enough confidence to sign my name to my opinion, I will be happy to provide it. They respect that.

TOP FIVE QUESTIONS TO ASK SELLERS DURING A LISTING APPOINTMENT

Have you had this property on the market before?

What criteria will you use to hire an agent?

If I show you how I can maximize the sale of your property and answer all of your questions, are you prepared to list today?

Tell me about your last experience with an agent when selling property. What could that agent have done to improve his or her service? What did you like best about the service you received?

Last and most important: When your property sells, what are you going to do next?

During every appointment, I find out what sellers have in mind in terms of pricing their properties. I might simply ask, "What do you think the offering price of your property should be?" Alternatively, you could ask, "Are there any recent sales in the area that I should pay special attention to in arriving at a suggested offering price for your property?"

In most cases, the seller is reluctant to divulge his or her feelings regarding the offering price. Nearly every time I ask either question, the answer is "We have done no research, are aware of no comps, and have no idea whatsoever what is going on in the market. This is why we called you. We need your expert advice."

These same folks, by the way, suddenly become experts on every sale that has taken place within a 20-mile radius during the past 20 years once I finally deliver my price opinion. Miraculously, they can name names, dates, prices, square footages, acreage, and so on.

The last thing I ask during my first appointment is what criteria the seller will use in selecting an agent to market the property. I always want to know the questions they will ask "on the exam" before I actually take it. Yet, you'd be amazed how many agents never ask this fact-finding question of potential sellers.

The Second Listing Appointment

Once I've had a chance to view the property, review my notes, and check all the market data, I can present the comparative market analysis that I prepared after my first appointment.

For effectiveness, I suggest the listing presentation be given in both printed and PowerPoint formats.

As I go through my presentation using PowerPoint on my computer, I emphasize four or five of the unique selling propositions, USPs, that I and my company provide. I actually ask the seller to assign a value to each of these points of difference.

For example, when presenting my Ten-Page Checklist for Preparing the Property For Sale, I cover the concept and the benefits of this particular report. *Under no circumstances will I give away the report until the listing contract is signed.*

However, I will give the seller enough information about what it contains so I can ask, "Ms. Seller, how much extra value do you think we can create for your property in the marketplace if we execute this checklist?" Unlike in a court of law, agents are allowed to "lead the witness" during a listing presentation. Usually on the first USP discussion, sellers are perplexed about something so I help them by saying, "Do you think if we execute this ten-page checklist for preparing the home for sale that we might receive an extra one or two percent in sales price?" Explained this way, they usually concede one or two points.

I continue this process explaining my remaining three or four USPs, totaling between six and nine percentage points altogether. That's based on just these five differences that I and my company bring to the marketing process for a particular piece of real estate.

Again, leading the witness, I'll say, "So it looks like we agree that by listing with me, you're likely to receive as much as ten percent more for your property based just on the five unique selling points we bring to the marketing process. Are we in agreement on that?"

Draw a line through the number, whether it's six or ten, and then say, "Perhaps we should be more conservative and agree that, based on just these four or five things I do differently than others, I'm likely to help you realize five percent more for your property than any other agent or company." Once you have the seller's agreement on this, commission discussions become easier to deal with. Any time the seller talks about a reduction in fee, simply refer to the fact that you agreed your services will likely result in a 5% higher selling price.

If you think carefully about the listing presentation process, many agents "stress out" for days and hours before the appointment, wondering what the seller will ask and what the objections might be. Honestly, in my 35 years in the business, I rarely hear something new.

Several years ago, however, I was making a presentation to a delightfully charming 85-year-old woman who had the most beautiful blue eyes I'd ever seen. We delivered the prelisting package and did the first information-gathering appointment. Then I went through my whole marketing plan during the second appointment.

During the course of her married life, this wonderful woman had bought and sold high-end homes at least a dozen times. She said, "John, this all sounds very good. What I would like you to do now is take me to the front door of my house and show it to me as if I were the buyer." I thought I'd fall off the chair. I've never been asked anything like this before. I was caught totally off guard.

Nevertheless, during my first visit to the property, I noted her comments about the front foyer, the large closet, the high ceiling she had designed and built to give her smaller retirement home the feeling of the larger ones where she had lived for years. When I repeated this during our "showing," we hadn't gone past the foyer when she said, "That's quite enough. Let's sign the papers and get started."

What an offer she made! Imagine, after you reached the last slide of your PowerPoint, if you asked the owners to join you at the front door and show them their house as if they were potential buyers. What a great impression that would make! Imagine how surprised your competitors would feel if they were asked to do the same thing during their presentation.

With high-end listings, we typically contract for a minimum of six months and many times make the contract viable for a year. Selling cycles, even in good times, can be time-consuming because the field of potential buyers for high-end properties is not always huge. Plus we guarantee our work. If at any time the seller is dissatisfied with our services, we cancel the contract with no cost or obligation to them.

High-end real estate agents especially get into trouble when they fail to meet the expectations of their clients. To make sure this doesn't happen, instruct sellers on what their expectations should be during your listing presentation.

Here's how you'd explain the process:
- Say what will happen;
- Say who will make it happen; and
- Say when it will happen.

In this way, you prepare the seller for a quick sale or even the possibility of a drawn-out 18 months on the market, whichever you believe will most likely happen.

Then, in a similar way, you'd explain how many showings are likely to take place during what given point in time. State the likely ratio of Internet visits to inquiries to in-person inspections. Note that during certain times of year, traffic will be greater (or not), and so on.

On Cape Cod, for instance, many people are surprised to know that the three slowest weekends of the year tend to be Memorial Day, Fourth of July, and Labor Day. This runs contrary to intuition because on these weekends, large throngs of people visit our beautiful peninsula.

Remember, however, most buyers want their home bought, closed, renovated, and ready to go *before May*. Plus, these holidays are marked as family times, not necessarily real estate times.

However, no prediction is ever 100% right. I won't insinuate that no one will buy a house during these three summer weekends. Indeed, I remember being part of a tense bidding war during one Fourth of July weekend. Just understand the trends in your area.

People might also be surprised to know that the busiest weekends of the year for Cape Cod real estate tend to be Columbus Day, Veteran's Day, and even Thanksgiving weekend. After the December holiday season has past, we get busy again on President's Day weekend in February. In fact, most weekends during the late winter and early, early spring months attract activity. Be sure to inform your sellers of typical patterns in your area.

Bear in mind also that after the information gathering appointment, your second appointment where you actually present your marketing plan and market analysis may not take place on the property itself. In fact, it could take place rather far away and in front of several interested parties. I have done several listing presentations where I set up a small LCD projector and made my PowerPoint in front of a group.

LONG DISTANCE LISTING APPOINTMENTS

I remember one recent listing appointment where I traveled to New York City to meet in the boardroom of a large law firm. Before arriving at the law firm's offices, I was photographed and presented with a temporary ID to get me onto the elevator. Several people had gathered in the boardroom, including attorneys, trust officers, and heirs. In addition, a large speaker phone sat in the center of the table so that far-flung family members could listen in by telephone to hear my presentation. While I have done presentations in front of groups before, this was the first time a presentation included people who were off-site.

Doing such presentations shouldn't intimidate you, though. Make your same presentation and just imagine being in a comfortable kitchen presenting the way you do most of the time.

Lastly, it is important to give your clients regular written reports. High-end individuals are used to receiving them and won't be impressed if you skip that step.

8

SEVEN STEPS TO
THE RIGHT PRICE

PRICING, THE MOST IMPORTANT PART OF MARKETING ANY PROP-
erty, happens to be the most challenging part of being a luxury real
estate specialist.

You're not only dealing with a multimillion-dollar estate, but you're
also trying to get an eager client to agree on a price. In many cases,
you're pricing a one-of-a-kind estate for which comps are few and
far between, if they exist at all.

With rare exceptions, all the marketing in the world—including
multimillion-dollar ads during the Super Bowl—will not sell an over-
priced property.

And did I mention that high-end buyers tend not to throw money
around? In my market, all the turnip trucks are empty...no one is
falling off and overpaying for property.

On a recent visit to Naples, Florida, I stopped by the local Bentley
dealership to browse—one of my favorite pastimes. Prominently displayed outside the showroom was a perfect, four-door black Bentley
with a huge yellow sign hanging from the rearview mirror that read
"$30,000 Off."

Even wealthy people expect value in this economy!

THE EYE OF THE BEHOLDER

Magnificent homes and estates in the luxury market are unique—
only in rare cases are two comparable. Indeed, nothing could be
more unlike the typical homes located in a subdivision built by one
builder or developer than many high-end residences. Many times
in the same concentrated area, every home looks as if it could have
been designed by a different architect and built by a different builder.
Although they all may feature elements of local design, such as New
England architecture, similarities end right there.

All this adds to the pricing challenge because in many cases you're
comparing apples to oranges.

I often compare high-end homes to rare and beautiful works of
art. As a matter of fact, most sellers love this analogy. Think of how
difficult it would be to find comparables for the Mona Lisa or other
rare works of art. The same difficulty comes in finding comparables
for that 12,000-square-foot custom home on 18 waterfront acres.
Add to this the fact that sellers expect to receive a huge return for
the extravagant custom features they've added and you have a major
challenge on your hands.

While bowling alleys, expensive home theatres, gold-plated faucets,
and similar accoutrements dazzle and delight the property owner,
they likely won't have similar value to a prospective buyer who may
detest bowling, prefers reading over watching movies, and prefers
polished nickel fixtures over gold ones.

Years ago, I listed a home that had a custom-built wicker-trimmed
high-back armchair commode in the master bathroom. A sight to
behold. I have never had the pleasure of making use of such a customized creation, but it must be quite an experience. Needless to
say, all the potential buyers—including the ultimate purchaser of
the property—made removing this artifact the number one item on
their list. Clearly, it conveyed no value to the buyer.

Adding to the valuation challenge is that sellers may lack motivation to sell quickly. "We will sell the estate if we can get $25,000,000"
is a refrain often heard in high-end circles. If the stars line up, the
planets go retrograde, the tide comes in, and the moon is full, we
just might sell.

Low motivation makes for high prices.

Pricing becomes an even bigger challenge when the sellers of an estate property are second- or third-generation family of the original owner. They usually have grandiose plans for the proceeds of the sale. To start, they look for an offering price that's evenly divisible by the number of beneficiaries. We can always predict that, when there are four heirs, they'll want either $4 million or $8 million, three heirs either $3 million or $6 million, and so on. Their dreams and desires rarely have a connection to the reality of the marketplace.

So for the price you present to have any chance of being accepted by a seller, it must be delivered with conviction as well as being logical and well documented. Let's discuss how to accomplish these criteria.

COMPETITIVE MARKET ANALYSIS (CMA)

As mentioned earlier, high net worth individuals are used to dealing with experts who provide written reports, which usually include one-page executive summaries. In a competitive market analysis, they look for detailed arguments, supporting evidence, and a clear rationale for the value conclusion arrived at by the agent. And they'll only read all this detail once they scan the summary. Based on its logic and the depth of research behind it, they determine if the CMA warrants their time reading it.

When I was starting my real estate career as a young man, I lacked the credibility of the long-time practitioners who had gray hair and years of experience. As a way to make up for that, I took several appraisal classes and learned to construct a narrative appraisal for each of my CMAs. Included were hand-drawn floor plans, detailed listings of comparables, and painstakingly constructed adjustment grids—with no Excel spreadsheets to rely on back then!

The sales adjustment grid created in Excel (thank heavens for Excel today!) is a critical part of any CMA. Grids used by appraisers and the prepackaged CMA software are, in my opinion, unnecessarily detailed for my purposes.

For example, in a typical subdivision, a 1,500-square-foot home may sell for more than the neighboring home because of an additional half bath, an extra fireplace, or a finished basement. These items are all exactingly noted and their values calculated in a normal bank appraisal adjustment grid.

In luxury real estate, this level of detailed adjustment of the elements of comparison is not required. The main elements of comparison for high-end estate property include date of sale, square footage, condition, location, utility usability, and privacy. Many subheadings can be found under each of these major categories.

When I do a CMA, I use a simple spreadsheet (see sales adjustment grid that follows) that may have only eight or nine elements of comparison. I rarely adjust for differences in bedrooms, fireplaces, baths, or half baths, for instance.

CMA CORNERSTONES

The name of the luxury real estate game is this: preparation based on information.

This section provides the building blocks you need to create an effective CMA. Regarding reaching an agreement on an appropriate price between seller and agent, it's important to reiterate the seven steps you need to take before reaching that accord.

Step #1: On my first appointment with sellers, I explain my process for arriving at a suggested offering price for their property. In this first step, I:

- interview the owners using the questions from Chapter 7,
- examine the property carefully,
- measure all the rooms, and
- take copious notes as I inspect the property following the brief owner-guided tour.

Based on the information from my visit and inspection, I'm in a position to gather comparable data that truly are comparable.

Step #2: Next, I prepare the CMA document. Now, when I said that Step #1 involves finding comparable sales, I can almost guarantee that the seller will not think they are comparable. To "make" them comparable (or at least to diffuse the seller's argument), you need to adjust the sales prices of the comparable sales for the following seven elements:

1. Date of Sale: You can see from the spreadsheet shown that I do all of my adjustments as percentages rather than numbers. It is much easier to defend that the market is up (or down) 5% since "comparable sale number one" occurred than it is to say the market is up $100,000 for your property since the date "comparable one" sold.

2. Acreage: Like all of our adjustments, this is subjective. I like to combine privacy with acreage because that's what buyers in the high end mostly seek. Also, it's possible for some properties with one acre to have more privacy than a property with two acres. So if the home on which you are trying to establish value has one acre and one of the comparables has two acres, the land is not necessarily worth twice as much. I try to keep all percentage adjustments at 5%, 10%, 15% or 20%. If you require an adjustment of any one element of more than 20%, perhaps you need to look for a better comparable. Make large adjustments only as a last resort.

3. Location: We constructed our Location Matrix in Chapter 4 when we were becoming experts in the area. This is where it will come in handy. In fact, a copy of it should be a part of your CMA. Talk about impressive! Again, location is a percentage adjustment along the same lines as acreage.

4. Age/Condition: Appraisers have a concept they refer to as effective age. An 80-year-old home that has been rebuilt from the studs out with all new systems and finishes might have an effective age of five years where the comparable may be a two-year-old home that has an effective age of 20 years because of poor maintenance or abuse. Actual age is good to note in your CMA spreadsheet, but effective age, adjusted again by percentage, is critical.

5. Amenities: If the home on which you're working to establish value has a deep water dock or slope-side location or sandy beach while the comparable does not, you must make another percentage adjustment. As with all adjustments on the spreadsheet, the actual percentage is subjective; it's based on your

Sales Comparison Grid
123 Sample Street
Cape Cod, MA

	SUBJECT	COMPARISON 1			COMPARISON 2			COMPARISON 3		
ADDRESS	123 Sample Street Cape Cod, MA	234 North Street Cape Cod, MA			567 West Street Cape Cod, MA			890 South Street Cape Cod, MA		
PRICE		$6,000,000			$7,450,000			$7,600,000		
CURRENT ASSESSMENT*	$5,580,700	$5,580,700	107.5%		$3,584,000	207.9%		$4,871,500	156.0%	
SALES DATE		Nov-2008	-5.0%	($300,000)	Dec-2008	-5.0%	($372,500)	May-2008	-10.0%	($760,000)
LOT SIZE / PRIVACY	0.77	2.23 Acres	-15.0%	($900,000)	1.9 Acres	-10.0%	($745,000)	1.35 Acres	0.0%	$0
HOUSE SIZE (SQ FT)	4,567	5,123	12.2%	($166,800)	5,224	14.4%	($197,100)	8,362	83.1%	($1,707,750)
COST PER SQ FT**		$300			$300			$450		
AGE	1920 Eff 2007	1920 eff 2000	0.0%	$0	1998 eff 2007	0.0%	$0	2002 eff new	-10.0%	($760,000)
FLOOR PLAN	Cape	Stucco	0.0%	$0	Cape	0.0%	$0	Cape	0.0%	$0
CONDITION	Excellent	Very Good	10.0%	$600,000	Excellent	0.0%	$0	Excellent	0.0%	$0
LOCATION	Sample Hood	Seaville	15.0%	$900,000	Goose Harbor	-20.0%	($1,490,000)	Egg Island	10.0%	$760,000
VIEW	South Bay	North Bay	0.0%	$0	West Bay	0.0%	$0	North Bay	0.0%	$0
WATERFRONT	South Bay	North Bay	0.0%	$0	West Bay	0.0%	$0	North Bay	0.0%	$0
DOCK	"L" Shaped Deep Water	"L" Shape Deep	0.0%	$0	Interior	5.0%	$372,500	Interior	5.0%	$380,000
BEACH	Some Sand	na	5.0%	$300,000	na	5.0%	$372,500	North Bay	0.0%	$0
GARAGE	3 Attached–Living Space Above	na	5.0%	$300,000	3 Attached	0.0%	$0	3 Attached	0.0%	$0
APARTMENT		na	0.0%	$0	na	0.0%	$0	na	0.0%	$0
BOATHOUSE	Separate Guest Cottage	Guest Cottage	0.0%	$0	na	15.0%	$1,117,500	Permit	15.0%	$1,140,000
POOL	Gunite	Gunite	-1.0%	($60,000)	Gunite	-1.0%	($74,500)	Gunite	-1.0%	($76,000)
OTHER	Tennis Court	na	-1.0%	($60,000)	na	0.0%	$0	na	0.0%	$0
OTHER	Not Winterized	HVAC	-2.0%	($120,000)	HVAC	-2.0%	($149,000)	HVAC	-2.0%	($152,000)
OTHER			0.0%	$0		0.0%	$0		0.0%	$0
TOTAL ADJUSTMENT				$493,200			($1,165,600)			($1,175,750)
ADJUSTED PRICE as of	August 1, 2009 ($5m to $11M)			$6,493,200			$6,284,400			$6,424,250

* Average Price to Current Tax Assessment: 157%
** Market cost per square foot for comparable construction quality

Total Number of Competing Offerings: 8   Number of Similar Sales in Past 12 Months: 4

There is currently a 2.0 year supply of competing offerings.

opinion, which is based on your knowledge and experience in that market.

6. Square footage: This one is easy. If the subject property is 10,000 square feet and the comparable has 8,000 square feet, you want to make an adjustment for the 2,000 square foot difference at the market cost per square foot of similar construction. Let's refer to when we were becoming experts in our market. We interviewed builders to get an idea of these costs. Here's where these cost estimates go.

7. Other: Other adjustments could be guest houses, boat houses, heli-pads, or landing strips. Again, most "others" are adjusted on an estimated cost basis.

Note: You can download a usable version of the spreadsheet in this chapter at www.jackcotton.com.

Step #3: In this step, I make comparisons. Once again refer to the research we conducted as part of becoming an expert in our market. Calculate the assessment ratio, comparable selling prices per square foot as well as absorption rate.

For example, you may find that the three comparable sales you considered sold on average for 112% of their assessed valuation. If the property you are working to value is assessed at $1 million, this ratio would indicate a selling price of $1.12 million. How does this number compare to the one you calculated using the spreadsheet? The numbers should be rather close. If they aren't, look for a problem in your assumptions regarding the adjustments.

I typically deliver this comparison, at the earliest, on my second appointment and possibly at a later date once a listing contract is signed.

Step #4: The second appointment with the seller is when I present the marketing plan and CMA. As part of this step, I make sure the seller knows that this suggested offering price remains confidential between me and the client. I assure the seller I'll tell no one, including my fellow agents, about our pricing discussion.

Step #5: The pricing committee from my office visits the property during its standard weekly tour. (Set up an office pricing committee simply by designating the people who can tour your listing with you that day—or whatever is customary in your office.) Each person on the pricing committee gives you his or her impression of what the offering price of the particular property should be.

Step #6: Discuss comments with the seller relating to what the pricing committee said and compare it with what was suggested in the CMA. Based on this input, the seller decides on the appropriate offering price. Then you decide whether to take the listing at that level.

Step #7: The final step of the process involves testing the offering price as it hits the market. As I point out clearly to the seller, the reaction to our value proposition of the multiple listing services (MLS) is like the reaction a barometer has to the weather.

For example, if the property goes on the market and in the first 24 hours we get several hundred agent views of the new listing but no calls to show it or no requests for information, we have our first indication that the price might be too high.

When the "public view" statistics are available from either our own web site or Realtor.com, this gives us a second indication of market acceptance of a value proposition. I once had a listing that showed 5,000 visits on Realtor.com in the first 30 days, but we fielded no requests to show it. This clearly indicated we'd missed the mark from a pricing standpoint.

It's critical that you explain this process to the seller on the first appointment. Otherwise, you run the risk of having that person think you were making up the rules as you go, when you report back during the marketing process, especially if there's a lack of activity.

SAMPLE CMA COVER LETTER

Every CMA should state your opinion of the fair market value of the subject property as of a Date Certain, as this sample letter shows:

> At your request, I have examined the above captioned
> property for the purpose of reporting to you my opinion of
> its fair market value as of _____ , 2010.

The next two paragraphs explain the definition of fair market value as well as the process used to compare the subject property with recent sales of similar properties and competing offerings.

Fair market value is the price at which the property would change hands between a willing buyer and willing seller, neither being under any compulsion to buy or sell, and both having reasonable knowledge of the relevant facts.

The most reliable means of estimating the fair market value of a given piece of property is through the comparison of recent sales and competing offerings of similar properties. No two properties are exactly comparable; nevertheless, this is the best method we have at our disposal. A summary of comparable sales and competing offerings are contained in this proposal.

The next paragraph sets the stage for testing the price with both our pricing committee and our monitoring of Internet activity.

We will test our offering price as your home goes on the market during our regular weekly office tour. After the tour, my fellow Company agents will give me their opinion as to what the offering price for your property should be. They will not be aware of our price discussion. We will talk once the numbers are in and finalize the price.

Remember, once we are on the market and have a number of showings with no offers, or if we don't get requests for showings, our offering price could be too high. MLS activity is the best "barometer" of the market's reaction to our value proposition.

When delivering a price opinion, always leave yourself an "out." There is nothing worse than having sellers call you months after a property has been on the market and after you've suggested one or two price adjustments. Then they bring out your original price opinion and say, "What about this? You're the one who suggested we start at this higher price." The following paragraph precludes this possibility by leaving us an "out."

The real estate market is in a constant state of change. Interest rate policies, inflation figures, and financial markets all have varying effects on the real estate market. It is important to review our price recommendation in the next four to six weeks to determine its relevance in the context of the market that exists at that time.

The last element of the CMA is the actual value conclusion. Again, because we are dealing with unique luxury properties, it's advisable to give the seller a range between which you think the property will actually sell. I'll often then give a third number that is no more than 10% above the high end of the range as the number two test of the market. That paragraph follows.

> I have made a thorough analysis of the market data contained herein.
>
> Based upon my experience in the marketplace and the market information available to me, it is my opinion that your property will sell for between $_____ and $_____ . If you plan to put your house on the market, I would suggest an initial offering price of $_____ to "test the market." After a reasonable time, we would discuss the need to address the price based upon market activity we have experienced.

Nobody can predict the exact selling price of any piece of real estate, let alone the unique property or estate. However, the process outlined herein will give you credibility with the seller, help you arrive at an accurate estimation of fair market value, and avoid running the risk of overpricing the property in the marketplace. You have also set the stage for price adjustments should they become necessary.

Accompanying my CMA (along with photos, maps, descriptions of recent sales and competing offerings), I include a sales comparison spreadsheet. It's a simple form illustrated in the following section.

The explanation here is similar to what I'd include in the body of my CMA to give details about my calculations to the seller.

SALES COMPARISON GRID EXPLAINED
In Appendix One, you can see a copy of an actual narrative accompanying a sales comparison grid.

Note: When doing a CMA, a qualified expert NEVER averages sales prices to arrive at an indication of fair market value. This statement may cause confusion, given that we often look at average sales prices, average assessment ratios, and so on. The distinction is that when looking at comparable sales, the qualified expert reconciles the market data into an indication of value.

Anyone can calculate an average. (You could probably train a circus chimp to do it!) However, your expertise comes in knowing the nuances of the market and how much weight to put on each comparable. For example, you may put the most weight on one of the comparables because it was located two doors away and sold within the last 30 days. State that fact in your value opinion. When discussing the CMA with your potential client, explain this concept and that you don't simply average the prices of comparable sales to estimate the value of the client's property. The true luxury expert reconciles the adjusted comparable sales data into a suggested offering price for the subject property.

9

LISTING
PREPARATION

AT ANY GIVEN TIME, ONLY A LIMITED NUMBER OF PEOPLE CAN afford multimillion-dollar properties. This is especially true in a challenging market.

Even in the category of high-end properties, buyers might have a dizzying array of choices. So put yourself in the mindset of a typical luxury buyer: *What would cause you to consider one property over another?*

First, you'd look at the seller's asking price. Just as important, you'd take note of the condition and the general impression of the property, either in person or online.

Your goal as an agent is to positively maximize the feeling that buyer gets when he or she enters the property you've listed. You want the buyer to feel comfortable, welcome, and at ease when inspecting the property.

I'm not saying your client needs to rebuild, renovate, or rehab the property before the listing enters the market. But I *am* saying that elements that create ambiance and special property features need to be shown in the best possible light. Remember, high-end listings to choose from always abound compared to the number of available qualified buyers. Your goal? Be so well prepared you move your list-ing to the top of the preferred list.

How? You may have heard a lot of buzz about the concept of stag-ing. I'm not a huge fan of the term "staging" because it can connote "contrived" or "not realistic," but I'll stick with it. Everyone in the business appears to have an understanding of what it means.

I highly recommend visiting the web site www.stagedhomes.com hosted by Barb Schwarz, the pioneer of home staging. It features a wealth of information about the concept of staging, preparing proper-ties for sale, and even the opportunity to take an online or in-person class that can lead to a designation in the skill and art of staging. At a minimum, buy her book *Home Staging: The Winning Way to Sell Your House for More Money.*

Any successful agent will tell you that homes that have been well-prepared for the market sell more quickly for higher prices and with less aggravation than those that aren't prepared. Doing so is a no-brainer.

DETAILS, DETAILS

As Will Rogers once said, "You never get a second chance to make a good first impression." Keep that in mind as you walk through the property, taking careful note of all elements beginning with the exterior and setting. (A detailed list I use to prepare property for the market appears at the end of this chapter.)

Be diligent and note answers to the following: How is the landscap-ing? Are parts of the home hidden by overgrown trees and shrubs? Are branches hanging over or actually touching portions of the dwell-ing? Do animals have easy access to the roof and chimney, or is sunlight being blocked from critical areas of the home?

We always recommend the seller get a major haircut for all trees, plants, and shrubs around the dwelling. With minor exceptions, all tree limbs should be far enough from the ground so that one can walk without having to duck.

Plantings and flowerbeds should be edged, mulched, and free of weeds. Even in the off season, displaying a sharp edge, fresh mulch, and neatly trimmed plants and shrubs makes a huge impression.

If attractive views can be seen from the property, trim trees and shrubbery to enhance them. However, you don't want to violate any local conservation rules or ordinances. Consult the authorities to obtain authorization to do this work. Nothing can hurt the marketing of the home like an enforcement order from a local regulatory agency.

We had a listing appointment at a water view estate a year or so ago. In order to enhance that all-important first impression, a family member decided to trim (hack) all the vegetation along the shoreline embankment. Of course, the local conservation commission found out because the "hacking" was visible. It resulted in a conservation enforcement order that required revegetating the embankment and regular inspections by the commission.

Enforcement orders are recorded at the registry of deeds much like a lien. They can often take a year to discharge (three years in this case). Do you see how this can possibly help in the marketing of a property? Of course not.

On the dwelling itself, make sure the front entry is clear and clean of mold, cobwebs, dirt, and debris. Driveways should be blown or swept clean; those made of gravel should be raked and gravel or stones added as needed.

Nothing looks worse than plant life growing from gutters. Seeing dark, vertical dirt lines in the gutters around a house is a sure sign that both the gutters and the downspouts may be clogged and need to be cleared.

Many agents suggest power washing older or moldy shingles before the property goes on the market. I am leery of this; power washing can do major damage to shingles, especially ones that are older. You can accomplish a much better look with a low-power wash of TSP (trisodium phosphate) or a light solution of bleach. Your best bet is to check with painting contractors. They're most often the best resources for this kind of work.

Check the roof. Be aware that some architectural shingles installed 15 to 20 years ago are prone to the growth of mold and algae that can cause discoloration and streaks. This is especially true on light-colored roofs. Again, a low-pressure wash can solve this problem.

THE INSIDE

Once inside the home, be aware of any odors. I've been to homes, even expensive ones, where the smell hit me in the head like a hammer when I walked through the doorway. Although smoking has become less prevalent in our society, your seller may be a smoker. When the property is on the market, enforce a rule that everyone must smoke outdoors or at least in the garage. Unpleasant odors from smoking or pets would require all carpets in the dwelling to be cleaned.

Windows should be washed inside and out, floors waxed and polished, and ceilings inspected for cracks, discoloration, and signs of non-active leaks.

Turn your attention to clutter. Explain to your sellers that they'll move sooner or later, so they might as well begin the task of getting rid of their unused items. Closets, drawers, cabinets, attics, under-eave storage spaces—all of these look better when they're free of clutter.

Take a fresh look at the furniture arrangement in each room. Many times there's just too much furniture! Suggest that some of the largest pieces be removed and sold or put into storage. I suggest "taking charge" and rearranging seating and other areas throughout the house to take best advantages of views—whether they're of water, mountains, open space, or conservation areas visible from within the rooms.

Check to see that all fireplaces are cleaned and especially that the creosote, soot, and other debris are cleaned from the glass.

Be sure high-watt bulbs are installed in all fixtures for maximum brightness, taking care never to install a bulb that has more wattage than the fixture is designed to accommodate. Bear in mind that on some of the days you're showing the property, it will be dark and gloomy outside. The brighter you can make the home inside during these days, the better.

I once toured an expensive, newly constructed waterfront home that featured 12,000 square feet of beautifully designed and executed construction. The artwork was unforgettable—paintings and statues of nude women wherever I looked. While I thoroughly enjoyed walking around, when I shifted to my "buyer's eyes," I realized how much that artwork could distract a potential buyer. If I were the agent for that home, I would find different art work, even if I had to borrow it from a local artist or gallery. Similarly, posters, pictures, and some artwork found in teenagers' rooms could be shocking to a viewer. I recommend encouraging sellers to put away items that might be distracting during the time the house is on the market.

Another more traditional waterfront mansion had a portrait of a woman over the fireplace. I learned about the strict instructions—passed from owner to owner—to never remove that painting or the woman's ghost would not be at all pleased. We had to balance this against the creepy feeling buyers had as her eyes "followed" them around the room. We did sell the house, and the buyer took our advice and instruction seriously. The portrait remains to this day.

Another time several years ago, we listed a large waterfront house with an extensively finished series of basement recreation rooms. Throughout this lower level were dozens of taxidermied animals from the owner's numerous hunting trips to Africa. One room featured animals of all sizes, including the requisite roaring lion's head and opened-mouth alligator. Most disturbing, however, was the life-size Bambi-like deer standing in the corner of the room.

All of this taxidermy needed to be removed eventually, so we told the seller it was pointless to put this property on the market unless every piece was gone before the first showing took place. You may think that a seller will be offended or resistant to this kind of advice or instruction. One great thing about most high-end sellers is that they made their wealth by understanding money and marketing. If your advice means more money to them, they will listen with kind attention.

Check and repair all leaky faucets and any stains they may leave in sinks, tubs, and showers. Clean, de-clutter, and sweep both the basement and the garage. If the seller wants to go the extra mile, painting floors and walls of both the garage and the basement goes a long way to making the property look its best. Toward that end, I recommend vacuuming the tops of all pipes and duct work in and around the basement and crawl spaces.

I have seen homes where the seller expects more than $20 million because of the location and extraordinary craftsmanship and finish in the interior. I then visit the basements and am horrified. In one, I expected a mummy to appear, or at least a stray critter or two.

Another expensive and beautifully detailed residence had hanging wires, dripping pipes, and debris in the basement. Some high-end sellers have never gone down to their basements, but potential buyers and their representatives certainly will.

People all spend lots of time in their kitchens—and so will the new owners. Give the kitchen in the home you're about to list special attention. Obviously all appliances, especially ovens, warming drawers, and microwaves, should be thoroughly cleaned and kept that way during the time on the market. In my experience, in a high-end home, the appliances are more for show than for actually cooking.

Look for cracks in the corners, clean out all drawers and cabinets so there appears to be lots of room for more. Put absolutely everything away that can be put away. Suggest the seller obtain small baskets or trays to contain small items used regularly rather than have them strewn around the countertops. Also check for loose cabinet door and drawer handles as well as finger marks and scratches around all handles. Repair and clean them as necessary.

You may think I'm overdoing it with this level of detail if you assume that most high-end homes are kept in impeccable condition. Not always true. I remember going to a prelisting appointment at a multi-million-dollar waterfront home. Stepping into the kitchen, it seemed by all appearances that the owners had left in the middle of eating lunch. I saw plates, dishes, and milk cartons left out on the counters as well as partially filled dishes and bowls and food items everywhere. But get this. The owners had left not two minutes ago; they'd left two and half months earlier. What a sight—and smell—to behold!

CONSERVATION COMPLIANCE

If the listing is likely to be under the jurisdiction of any type of conservation agency or organization, make sure all the paperwork is up to date and recorded as necessary.

For example, in listing properties in the Commonwealth of Massachusetts, agents and buyers often are excited about the deep water boat dock that may be a part of the offering.

What sometimes happens is that a seller applies for the necessary permission to build a dock or structure and neglects to get the certificate of compliance or meet the certificate of conservation obligations.

Over the years, the dock grows—a float in this direction, an extra ramp in that direction. Then, when the property sells, someone goes to get the certificate of compliance, but the existing dock doesn't match what was noted in the original plan. A deal can go up in smoke because of this oversight. At the very least, it can result in a massive renegotiation of a price and a delay in the closing that can take months or even a year while paperwork is brought into compliance.

If you think that the conservation commission is fun to deal with in general, try dealing with it when you have a large sale on the line.

Always check to see if any kind of conservation resource area, whether it be a stream, conservation forest, wetland, or other area affects your property. Make sure that if any work has been done, the appropriate authorities know about it, inspected it, and signed off on it!

In a case like this, I suggest you let the seller know this documentation is required to close a sale in writing. You can add it to the checklist of items the seller needs to complete to prepare the property for market. This way, you create a paper trail that may be helpful down the road if the property doesn't sell and the seller blames you, the agent, when in fact he or she hasn't executed all the items on your list. Take the opportunity to provide a gentle reminder whenever appropriate.

PREPARING FOR PHOTOGRAPHY

Once the home has been properly staged and repaired, it's time to schedule a photography session.

To produce the best possible listing brochures and Internet tour for a seller's home, do the following before the professionals arrive to photograph the home.

EXTERIOR

♦ Clear the property of lawn equipment, toys, and debris, both front and rear yards.

- Clear lawn and gardens of leaves and fallen branches.
- Close the lid on the grill and open any deck or patio umbrellas, no matter what time of year.
- Close all garage doors.
- Put cars in the garage or in the driveway as far back from the house as possible.

INTERIOR
- Turn on all lights to make home as bright as possible.
- Open all window cover-ups and shades completely.
- Clear all unnecessary items from countertops.
- Make sure beds are made and unnecessary items removed from floors and doorways.
- Put down all toilet seat covers.

While you may have dozens of showings of qualified buyers to your high-end listing, it is not always so. That's why the home must look its best during every showing opportunity. Share the following checklist with your seller to put everyone on the same team in having the property prepared for showings. If your seller is an absentee owner, make him or her aware that you'll be executing this list before the property is shown.

I recently brought potential buyers into a contemporary dwelling overlooking one of the largest lakes on Cape Cod. We walked in the front door to meet the listing agent. I saw the lights on but the blinds were drawn on the huge palladium-type window open to the view. I raced over to open the blinds. However, the impact of opening the front door and seeing the shimmering blue waters of the lake as part of the first visual image was lost.

SHOWTIME
Here are some last-minute touches to ask your sellers to take care of so they can make their homes look and sound appealing for the right buyers.
- Open drapes and window shades.
- Open all doors between rooms, to give an inviting feeling.
- Turn on all lights, including lamps.

90

◈ Turn off all TVs and other electronics.

◈ Tune the radio to a classical station or put a classical CD in the player but keep it low as background.

◈ Look around for clutter, including newspapers and magazines, and clear it away.

◈ See that the kitchen counters are free of unnecessary items and any dirty dishes are washed and put away.

◈ Empty trash containers.

◈ Take pets for a walk or ride in the car and take care of their food and/or litter area.

◈ Make sure beds are made and clothes picked up.

◈ Make sure bathrooms are clean, with towels folded and the toilet lid down.

◈ Make the house smell good! Place bowls of potpourri in some of the rooms and/or have something baking in the oven (bread is always good).

◈ If it's fireplace season or you have a gas log, light the fire if possible.

◈ It is very important for you to be away from the house and property during showings. Buyers will not "open up" to us if you are around.

Tell your sellers that whenever they depart from the house in the morning or during the day, to leave it as if they're sure it will be shown that day. Yes, this request is difficult sometimes. It might even mean getting up early to take care of these important items listed. But persuade them by saying, "You never know when the right people will look at your home so always be ready for them."

Your job is to give the house a quick look over before potential buyers arrive. Recently, I noticed a half-eaten fish lying on the living room fireplace hearth of a waterfront home. It seems that an osprey had lunch on the chimney and dropped the uneaten remains down to the fireplace hearth below. See how all your staging work can come undone in a matter of minutes?

10

MARKETING THE
LUXURY ESTATE

At your fingertips are a myriad of tools to grab the attention of those interested in high-end real estate: the Internet, newspaper and magazine ads, brochures, mailings, photos, and flyers. However, these tools are effective only if you know how to use them. This chapter helps you prepare your message so your marketing campaigns won't flounder. (Specific aspects of marketing—print advertising, the Internet, open houses, direct mail, and international marketing—are discussed in the marketing chapters that follow.)

Where Do High-End Buyers Come From?

Rather than guessing, it's good practice to conduct market research to determine where the high-end buyers in your area tend to come from. For example, we know that upwards of 85% of all buyers who ultimately purchase million-dollar properties on Cape Cod come from within a 25-mile radius of downtown Boston. The remaining 15% come from a variety of places in the world.

We also know that typical high-end Cape Cod buyers are in their upper 50s and have kids who are halfway through or nearly finishing college. One or both partners in the family have worked extremely hard to arrive at being able to buy the property being marketed.

For many of these buyers, their second-home resort property becomes a magnet that draws family together during the high season. Remember I mentioned that weekends, especially over Memorial Day, Fourth of July, and Labor Day, can be slow for home sales? This is why.

Recently, I was curious about specific characteristics of buyers of luxury real estate in my area. As you know, 2008 ended as a highly tumultuous year economically, especially in the real estate category. So I examined data on all buyers who had purchased homes in our area, whether through our agency and or another company. It was interesting to find out that 85% of the buyers of properties of $1.6 million and up came from the financial services industry.

I won't speculate on what this means, although I've noted that the trend continued through 2009. One might wonder if these folks were converting their financial assets into real estate assets. Whatever the reason, knowing this characteristic proves useful when crafting a marketing plan. Perhaps it means we should send brochures to executives in the financial service industry or market in specific financial trade publications. Maybe we need to look out for professions that dominate the purchases of high-end homes going forward.

BUDGETING EXPENSES

Agents often ask how much money they should commit to marketing a high-end listing. The answer varies and, of course, depends on the commission rates and splits as well as to what extent your company specializes in marketing high-end listings.

Any well-run real estate company sets a goal of committing 4% to 5% of gross commission income toward its marketing efforts. In reality, companies often find themselves committing a higher percentage because it's easy for marketing dollars to "run away" from you.

On top of marketing by their company, agents typically go above and beyond with mailings, brochures, and advertising on their own. The budget varies from agent to agent, but I've known many who spend 10% to 18% of their projected commission on additional marketing.

When calculating your budget, keep in mind that not every listing you have results in a sale. Know your ratio of listings taken to listings sold. For instance, say your ratio is three listings taken to one sold.

Assume the one sale would generate a $50,000 commission. You would allocate 10% or $5,000 gained from the commission of selling that one home and use that amount to market all three listings.

HAVE A PLAN

Whether you create your plan from an available program, design one in a spreadsheet, or use sticky notes on a board, you need a plan that's consistent, both in its design and its execution.

I am a big fan of real estate contact management software with action plans that can be designed, stored, and implemented for each listing. That means every time a property is listed and the plan is executed, the appropriate person will be alerted (through electronic reminders) to execute whatever piece of the marketing plan is due that particular day. Being forgetful at times, I find these ticklers extremely helpful.

CATCHING THE BIG ONES

Often when I talk to agents about marketing to owners and potential owners of high-end real estate, I draw comparisons to fishing. Unfortunately, many real estate agents prospect the way amateurs fish.

If you think about a large body of water that contains fish of all sizes and descriptions, many agents perch themselves on the shore, wharf, even in a boat, and cast or troll haphazardly. They hope their lure catches the interest of a passing fish that takes the hook. Please don't interpret this as being critical of fishermen; I enjoy fishing and find it relaxing.

In fact, I think *catching* a fish complicates the whole enterprise. When my kids were younger, I'd shave the barbs off the hooks so we could enjoy our time fishing without the messy "distraction" of bringing a fish into our boat to bleed and spew guts all over our freshly oiled teak deck.

For most people, though, the goal is to catch a fish or two. Likewise in the realm of luxury real estate. Out on the ocean, a novice fisherman looks across the expansive sea with no idea how to spot a school of fish lying under the surface. On the one hand, with the advent of electronics, they do have ways of looking beneath the boat to see if fish are present. On the other hand, experienced fishermen know how to look out on the water's surface and spot the telltale signs of a school of fish beneath. Whether it's the line of a shoal where fish like to feed or the smell and sight of a slick showing they're already feeding, schools of fish constantly leave clues.

The same is true of high net worth individuals. They like to travel together, not in packs or schools, but around people like themselves.

Similarly, like an experienced fisherman, an experienced luxury real estate professional knows how to find high net worth individuals where others look and do not see.

How can you be assured of "dropping your line" in the right place?

One marked difference between fishing for actual fish and fishing for high net worth prospects is that those prospects swimming in the water don't have gatekeepers. As explained in Chapter 18 on sphere of influence marketing, your database should be full of people who have direct access to high net worth individuals, circumventing their gatekeepers.

Let's examine who would typically fit the category of high net worth "fish" you're trolling for.

CHIEF EXECUTIVE OFFICERS

Prospecting for CEOs is the obvious no-brainer of the luxury real estate practice. Start by making a list of corporations within a reasonable radius of your market area, say 400 miles. Generally, the names and contact information of not only the CEOs but the top executive tier of these companies are available online and in the library.

For example, numerous directories such as Standard & Poor's, The Wall Street Journal, or Hoovers.com allow you access to the names of and contact information for executives, especially in publicly traded corporations.

Finding CEOs in private corporations can present more of a challenge, but you'll often find the information through local or regional business publications. It's not easy, though, to find information on owners of small companies.

Recently, I had an issue with the closing of a small property. We could not get a release from the lender, which happened to be one of the largest publicly traded banks in the world. I found it easy to get the private email address of the CEO using the resources just mentioned, send a message, and solve the problem in a few hours.

Contrast this with a recent complaint I had with my son's bicycle. The manufacturer is not a publicly traded company; it was next to impossible to track the CEO.

You can take the time to painstakingly think about each CEO you target and possible connections you may have to each of them. However, an easier and faster approach is to contact CEOs via direct mail. (Chapter 11 discusses direct mail in detail.)

TRADE SHOWS

Trade shows are an often overlooked means of promoting your business and your listings.

For years, our agency had a booth at the regional boat show. Our displays featured the waterfront properties we were listing. Typically, a spouse agrees to tag along to boat shows (or golf shows or tennis shows) to be a good sport, but doesn't show the same enthusiasm for the given theme. I guarantee that when these spouses come across your display of high-end real estate, they will stop and say, "Meet you back here in 45 minutes, honey," and thus you'll connect with a potential client for life.

Boat shows as well as golf and tennis expositions are just a few venues where you can set up displays of your real estate offerings. Also look for trade shows for various professions and attend them as a guest, an exhibitor, or a presenter.

Check with your local meeting or planning organizations to get schedules of groups of CPAs, attorneys, bank trust officers, physicians, or executives who will be meeting in the near future. Offering your services as a presenter of information they care about at one of the sessions can get you in front of a high net worth audience.

BUSINESS PROFILES

Whether it's in the *The Wall Street Journal*, *Forbes*, *Business Week*, or a local or regional business publication, you can read profiles of CEOs and other executives on a regular basis. The profiles share a lot about the person, not just the business he or she leads. This type of prospecting is highly effective because the person featured demonstrates an openness to being contacted—or wouldn't have allowed the profile to be done in the first place.

How do you approach these featured executives? Make a high-quality copy of the article or magazine cover, have it laminated on quality stock that features your name and logo with the word "Congratulations" at the top. Then mail or hand deliver it to the subject who was featured.

Here's a suggested way to work the cover letter:

> Dear Featured Executive:
>
> Your profile today in the *Regional Business Journal* was quite interesting. I am inspired by people who reach high levels of success and want to commend you on your achievement.
>
> Enclosed is an extra copy of the article, which I took the liberty of laminating for you.
>
> I represent a wide range of high net worth individuals and help them make property ownership decisions, which include tax planning, property tax reduction, and annual evaluations.
>
> In hopes that you have time to offer some advice as I market the most extraordinary properties in Luxuryville, I'll be giving you a call at your office in the next couple of days.
>
> Once again, congratulations. Sincerely,
>
> Larry Luxury Agent

INSIDER TRANSACTIONS

Executives and officers of publicly traded corporations must notify the U.S. Securities and Exchange Commission (SEC) with their intent to buy or sell stock in the companies to which they are connected. Fortunately for agents in the luxury market, these notifications are public information and can be found in The Wall Street Journal, Barron's magazine, or various web sites including insider-monitor. com. Think of it this way: If an executive is liquidating $25 million worth of company stock, he or she may be motivated to invest in one of your listings.

AFFILIATION MARKETING

In an effort to garner referrals from local providers of services to high net worth individuals who can bypass gatekeepers, consider a program of affiliation marketing. It can be highly successful as a long-term project.

Begin your affiliate program by sending invitations to businesses and service providers who cater to wealthy individuals. Bring them into your office with a promise of wine and cheese and a free seminar on a topic like "Low-Cost High-Impact Ways to Promote Your Business in a Challenging Economy."

When I give this talk to these business people, I start with a brief outline of the benefits of sphere of influence marketing. (The importance of sphere marketing for the luxury real estate agent is addressed in Chapter 18.) I talk about the track record of both myself and my company of reaching high net worth individuals and making sure all of our clients knew about the offerings of the people gathered. I invite each of them to provide me with 50 professionally produced one-page flyers or brochures about their business. My promise is that each time I receive an inquiry or close a transaction, the potential buyer will receive a folder with a map of the area and the information from each of those businesses that signed on to my affiliate program. Also, when I do regular mailings to my customer base, I include offerings from interested participants on a rotating basis.

I tell them I could easily charge for this service but all I ask in return is that they refer me to their high-end clients and include *my* one-page flyer with their own client mailings.

One time, we actually took this program one step further by dedicating a wall within our office located in the boutique-lined main street of our village, Osterville. The top of the wall had a sign that read "The Best of Osterville." Under the sign was a laminated advertising board (11″× 15″) for each of the business people who agreed to participate. We wanted people to browse our gallery and look with interest at these advertising boards created by our marketing department.

In return, we asked each merchant to feature one of our laminated display boards (12″× 15″) in a prominent location within their business. You could actually make them smaller, say 8.5″× 11″; my only suggestion is that you will gain maximum impact with similar sizes and branding of these display boards in your market.

As you can imagine, the first reaction among potential affiliates is the fear of alienating others they know in the real estate business by featuring us. I respond to that by saying: "While we would like an exclusive agreement, if someone else offers the same program, go ahead, and put their display board next to ours." Saying this worked to garner a "yes" about 80% of the time. And I can assure you that not once did any competitor come up with a similar display board to sit next to ours.

Imagine the impact of new arrivals to your village or town when they go from business to business, professional to professional, and keep seeing your name and your company's. Also, if you were driving business to your fellow merchants within your town, they would naturally want to reciprocate to build good will.

BROCHURES

The cornerstone of any high-end real estate marketing plan is, of course, the brochure describing the property. Depending on the size of the house and the offering price, you decide whether two, four, or more pages are appropriate. For most "entry-level" luxury properties, a two-page brochure is sufficient, while special properties can require four or more pages.

Start by developing a template to give all your brochures a similar look and feel. Your company and contact information needs to always be in the same place on the brochure so people can find it easily.

To produce a great brochure, you need fabulous photographs. While many agents take great pride in their photographic abilities, honestly, most photos taken by agents lack the quality required.

Perhaps a regular point-and-shoot camera shot of the exterior will be fine for your CMA photograph. However, for brochure photos, use a single-lens reflex digital (SLR) camera with the highest possible resolution. Also have a wide-angle lens and one or more external flashes with manual overrides handy.

Interior photography of high-end homes can be a challenge. Even a high-powered flash purchased as an accessory to most high-end SRL cameras cannot light up a 25- to 45-foot room. Professional photographers set up multiple lights throughout the room that are wirelessly synchronized with the camera to provide even light.

Most high-end residences have spectacular views of water, mountains, woods, streams, and so on, so you want to feature a beautiful photo of the room with the views clearly visible through the windows. Without equalizing the light between the inside and the outside, you either get a really bright window with a dark room or a great looking room with an over-lit window.

I've never been a fan of virtual tours or 360-degree panoramic views of listings online. They can take a long time to load, causing impatient web visitors to click away from your web site. Some versions require the user to add a plug-in, a step that's the kiss of death because visitors to your site do not want to wait for the plug-in to download. And even if they have the patience, they will be leery of downloading an unknown program. Instead, present a series of well-composed, well-lit, fast-loading still photographs. It's the best way for a potential buyer to *quickly* get the feel of a listed property.

You can read books on how to photograph the interior of your high-end listing. My advice is to engage the services of a professional. It will pay off in the long run.

Here's a new technique used by professional photographers. They set up a tripod in the featured room and program the camera to take 10 to 12 automatic exposures of the same shot with slightly different light settings. They then take those images back to their computers and use software to select the best elements from each photo. In this way, they make a master photo of unmatched quality. One caveat: The photos can look so perfect, they don't even seem real. In these situations, pay close attention to make sure this "too-perfect-to-be-real" effect doesn't occur.

When photographers use photo editing software, it's not ethical to make structural changes in the photograph, in my opinion. Adding trees, eliminating trees, removing wires, enhancing views, and similar changes are simply bad practice.

While proper light-equalized interior shots can be taken at almost any time of the day or in any weather, taking good exterior photographs often requires multiple visits. Note the orientation of the structure you plan to shoot so that the front elevation can be taken with full sun behind you. If there's a view from this property that you want featured, you'll be able to shoot the scene using the same sun position.

However, the rear elevation has to be shot later in the day when the sun is in a different position, lighting up the opposite side of the property. It's common to make two or three visits to get the lighting just right on a high-end property.

In the higher latitudes of the United States, autumn and winter exterior shots pose challenges because of the sun being low in the sky, creating long shadows. We partly solve this by maintaining a database of stock exterior shots of all important waterfront listings in our market. This also lets us use a summer photo even if the property comes on the market in winter.

Many people like to feature aerial photographs, especially for large properties. We do this from time to time, but the main goal of an aerial photograph is providing context. Most people don't view properties from the air so I rarely, if ever, use an aerial shot as my main photograph.

Instead, I prefer to rent a bucket truck or set up a ladder to shoot from an elevation high enough to "see" over trees and other tall features. This can show the view in the background without having to hire an aircraft.

WRITE COPY FOR VARIOUS OUTLETS

Whether it's for your web site, brochures, or print ads, writing good copy is a critical component of good marketing. Remember, you're dealing with educated, highly accomplished individuals who are immediately turned off by poor grammar, punctuation, and spelling. While I consider myself a decent writer (sometimes the flowing prose I write for a particular listing amazes even me), I usually opt for the services of a professional writer who can hone copy into perfectly succinct, descriptive text. Even Hemingway used an editor.

I'm always amazed at the simple, clean writing I receive from a professional copywriter. Descriptions that have been elegantly written are worthy of admiration. And they're so simple, you wonder why you couldn't think of them yourself!

Execute Templates

Be sure to have similar formats that build on your brand through repeated use of the unique graphic image you've developed. You can hire a professional to design the initial templates and then have a junior person drop photographs and copy into these templates at a lower cost than paying an experienced designer.

When creating templates for both brochures and ads, remember that less is more. *Their goal is to entice prospective buyers to visit the property.* Providing too much information can eliminate the need for many perspective buyers to visit the property in person.

This is why I'm not big on producing videos for high-end listings. They simply show too much, plus one can never capture the feeling of being on the property from a video or a photograph. Again, your goal is to get potential buyers to come to the property in person. Rarely will you sell a property sight unseen.

Years ago, we had the idea to create a hardcover brochure for a single-family residential listing—a huge and overly expensive endeavor. I will say the graphic product was beautiful but not worth the cost. We won an award for real estate marketing innovation and were admired by the real estate community. At the same time, I don't think it had any direct bearing on the ultimate sale of the home. And even though other potential sellers may have contacted us as a result of the hard cover, the effort was too extensive and expensive to duplicate.

Today, it's a different story. With web-based technology provided through sites like Shutterfly.com and Snapfish.com, a hardcover brochure for a single-family residential listing can be created quickly and easily. Start by selecting a template so you can print as many copies of the hardcover brochure as you want. They run about $35 per copy from Shutterly.com. With that information, you can decide when it's appropriate to use hard covers for your marketing.

We printed one hundred for a recent invitation only open house for neighbors of a waterfront estate. They were extremely well received; people just don't throw them away. I still see them occasionally at area homes I visit.

Whatever way you produce your brochures and ads, be sure they make a great impression.

Be sure to add a home book for each listing to your marketing plan. It's a beautifully designed, high-end binder that contains all the necessary details any buyer would want to know when viewing the property. Having a binder of plans, seasonal photographs, restrictions, deeds, maps, and so on certainly helps extend the length of the time a prospective buyer spends at the property. Make it impressive, too!

DIRECT MAIL

DIRECT MAILING BROCHURES TO PEOPLE YOU KNOW IS ADDRESSED in Chapter 9. This chapter provides ideas for direct mail campaigns to people you don't know.

WHERE TO SEND DIRECT MAIL

Many companies provide mailing lists broken down into a dizzying array of categories: businesses, professions, residents of homes assessed at certain values, people in certain zip codes, and on and on. If you're contemplating the purchase of a mailing list, make every effort to discern the methods that were used to build and maintain that list—elements that are key to the accuracy of the list.

For example, a list based on the telephone book may miss owners of expensive property who have unlisted numbers. Keep in mind, though, that no matter how the list is constructed, errors exist. When mailing in my desired geographic area, I shy away from purchased lists in favor of creating my own.

Your list can be created by accessing the tax assessor's records for the particular town in which you wish to work. Being familiar with the area puts you in a position to "clean" the list before sending mailings. I can assure you that sending a letter to an elderly couple in which one spouse has recently passed away is problematic. It's one sure way to give your marketing, your image, and your business a setback. Changes in family situations, such as divorce, also affect the accuracy of mailing lists. Be warned: not correcting a local mailing list can be hazardous to your business. This is why you need to be in tune with your market. Check records at your town hall for births, deaths, and divorces. You can also do Google searches for names on your mailing lists.

A potential issue with mailing lists based on assessor's records is that tax bills aren't always sent to the address of the property in your market. This is especially true in resort and second-home markets. Although it's an arduous task, you need to go over each and every person on your local list to make corrections.

Also, check to see if tax bills are being mailed to third-party payers, trustees, or other locations. When this is the case, I chance mailing to the physical address of the property and use first-class postage. For incorrect addresses, you receive the articles back. That tells you further research is required to confirm those addresses.

In addition to looking at assessor's tax records of the desired area, as an adventurous luxury real estate expert, you can visit towns likely to generate buyers to your area. In days gone by, we would travel to the western suburbs of Boston, spending hours in the local tax office creating lists based on owners of property above certain assessed value thresholds in towns known to generate a lot of buyers to our area. These days, you might be able to purchase such information from the town directly or from list brokers and dealers.

Keep in mind the categories of prospects we discussed earlier for purchasing or creating your own list. Whenever you see publicity about high net worth individuals connected to your area, add them to your master database—immediately.

Lastly, consider geographic areas close to you from which buyers tend to "move up." As an example, over time people who live on beautiful streets near the water may attain enough resources to move to the waterfront. For that reason, when sending direct mail about a new waterfront listing, I include high-end, non-waterfront areas in addition to those already on the water.

WHAT TO SEND

As emphasized throughout this book, every breath you take, every move you make must reflect the quality of the service and product that you provide. That means no sloppy, low-quality mailers or generic addresses like "occupant" or "homeowner."

In the early days of my real estate career, much hadn't been invented yet. Mobile phones, pagers, fax machines, copiers, computers, and word processors did not exist. For me, the first high-tech piece of equipment that transformed my ability to send direct mail was the IBM Selectric II typewriter with lift-off correction tape. Before the Selectric, I had to hand type 100 letters personalized to each recipient on my old Smith Corona typewriter. Typing errors had to be corrected with whiteout squares placed between the ribbon and the error on the page and struck over and retyped. Because they showed up in the finished product, often the letter had to be pulled from the typewriter and thrown in the corner with a pile that increased in size as the evening wore on.

With the IBM Selectric II typewriter and its lift-off tape, errors could be lifted off the page and retyped without a trace. Amazing! The pile of crumpled up letters in the corner shrunk.

Both then and now, all letters sent to high net worth individuals had and have to be personalized, no further discussion.

Think of your targeted recipient who is busy and probably receives lots of mail. Forget mailing labels. Addresses typed on the envelope and applied postage stamps make mail look much more personal and appealing to open than labeled and metered mail.

Remember, everything you mail needs to carry a value to the recipient. You may answer a question such as what is happening with values in your area at the time, what is predicted in relation to values, and so on. Providing valuable information makes your letter more likely to be read and establishes you as an expert, which is your goal.

In my experience, the best "hook" to capture readers is a question. That raises their natural curiosity. They want answers to the question posed. For example:

◆ Have you thought about whether your property tax assessment is accurate?

◆ What will you do if the new ordinance regulating deep water piers is enacted?

These topical questions pertain to a specific market. You can easily think of ones that pertain to your own.

Create a mailer that has staying power, or what's called shelf life. Give the recipient reason to hold on to what you've mailed. For example, an agent might send a calendar or sports schedules both for national and local teams. A popular and lasting mailer for our market was a tide chart. With the advent of the Internet, though, the value of a tide chart has gone out with, well, the tide.

As with a sphere of influence mailing, postcards can be used—but sparingly. The ideas discussed in this kind of marketing will make your postcards stand out from the norm. However, once again you're mailing to people you don't know. Items such as recipe cards, "how to choose a babysitter" postcards, and other cutesy type postcards aren't appropriate for high-end prospecting any more than they were for mailings to those you know.

The advantages of sending postcards, of course, include the ease of mailing, the lower cost of postage, and the ability to convey a message succinctly. They also provide a low-cost way to clean your mailing list. Once a year, send postcards to your entire list so you can see by those returned which addresses need to be updated.

Be sure that the themes of your postcard are local, local, local—aerial photos, seasonal landscape photos, local landmarks, works of art—these can work in your postcard mailings to high net worth individuals. You could also consider producing a postcard that depicts your market share. However, I think this information is better sent in a letter because a professionally address business envelope conveys more importance to the recipient than does a postcard.

Note that in our agency, we have rarely sent out CDs and have never sent out DVDs of our listings, although as times change, we may change our position. Why am I reluctant to send CDs and DVDs? The massive amount of information provided could give recipients reasons to eliminate a particular property before ever doing an in-person visit. Plus, as our world becomes increasingly high tech and impersonal, the experience of reading "real" personalized mail on quality paper will only increase in value and effectiveness.

For this reason, I have not fully converted to e-mail blasts—not so affectionately referred to as spam—as part of our direct mail prospecting strategy. E-mail is a great way to communicate with existing clients to keep them updated with marketing efforts undertaken on their behalf. In terms of prospecting for new business, however, I prefer "real" mail.

As with your sphere of influence mailing, have a plan. That means mapping out a calendar that delineates what you'll send, when you'll send it, and to whom you'll mail it. Direct mail can't be done in a haphazard fashion. Consistency of mailing is important. It may not be until the fifth or tenth time your mail is received that your image and message get imprinted in the mind of the recipient.

12

PRINT ADVERTISING

SOME AGENTS WANT TO INCREASE THEIR AVERAGE SALES PRICE, so they work in the high end. Others who are already successful in the high end want to gain ideas and techniques to improve their service. Yet other real estate professionals are happy dealing in lower price ranges but want to treat their clients like a million dollars. Ultimately, all professionals are well advised to give million-dollar service to all their clients. Print advertising still plays a strategic role in accomplishing this objective.

Advertising, in and of itself, is typically where agents or companies spend the majority of their resources and get the least amount of return—at least with respect to gaining actual buyers. Real estate offices can spend upwards of 80% of their marketing budget on print advertising. But when they measure their results, they often find that, at best, only 5% to 10% of their sales were initiated through that venue.

Print advertising has taken a backseat to other media, but it's not completely irrelevant. It's still a key part of a real estate professional's marketing arsenal. You need to be strategic in how you use it. It's the first thing that many sellers want, but it can zap a lot of your marketing energy to create and monitor print advertising. Additionally, it zaps a good chunk of your financial resources. The results just aren't there with haphazard ad placement, especially since online advertising took center stage.

You need laser-like focus on the goal of your advertising. Cost and effort are against you and they never back off. Therefore it's essential to find balance. I included this chapter to help you understand how to be the most efficient with your advertising resources. Use imagination, resourcefulness, and positioning. Create something that makes people want to call. Make it worth their time.

STATISTICS ON INTERNET USE TO FIND HOMES

According to The National Association of Realtors® Profile of Home Buyers and Sellers, *one-third of home buyers look online for properties as their first step in the home-buying process. About 87% of all home buyers and 94% of buyers ages 25 to 44 use the Internet to search for homes.*

My belief is that the higher you go in price range, the higher this percentage becomes.

THE PRINT ADVERTISING TRIAD

The purpose of an advertisement is to get people interested in what you have to offer. You want buyers to come in to your circle so you can qualify them and learn more about them and their motivations. For sellers, the objective is to find a Realtor® to represent the sale of their property. They often turn to print media, especially the newspaper, to see who has the biggest ads or the most ads or who's advertising in prominent papers such as *The Wall Street Journal*. That's who they call.

When buyers look at print ads, their main purpose is to eliminate properties from consideration. Think about the last time you searched for an item in print media. You scan the ads for keywords or "hot buttons" that catch your eye. If they don't match your criteria for what you're looking for, you cross them out as quickly as possible. Those ads don't qualify.

If you really want a business that provides a return and yields an income that's predictable and duplicable, you can't run it solely on advertising. It's just not going to work. You don't have enough money to buy business in this profession.

Ads are expensive, so make the ones you do create hit their mark using some foresight. I've identified three types of advertising that have varying degrees of success: property specific, institutional, and response.

PROPERTY SPECIFIC

Property specific is when you're advertising a beautiful waterfront estate on an exclusive street. You present a photo of the property, a description, and usually an "if you like this house give us a call" type tagline, otherwise known as a call to action. I say usually because I am often amazed at the number of ads I see with no call to action.

The problem with this advertising approach is that if you're a buyer who's not interested in that particular location or that particular body of water, if you like fresh water instead of salt water or bay water instead of ocean water, if you like a shingle style instead of a colonial—the list goes on—you're going to eliminate this particular ad from consideration.

As a result, property-specific ads can be too narrowly focused. In fact, they are the most expensive, least efficient form of advertising. Property-specific advertising is not going to serve the purpose of making your phone ring unless you hit that "one in a million" buyer who has to have this particular property.

INSTITUTIONAL

The institutional way of advertising is solely meant to promote the real estate company's brand and get buyers to keep it top of mind as well as drive ad viewers to the company's web site.

Picture a two-page spread featured in a prominent periodical. It shows only a dramatic photo of a spectacular dwelling, a company logo, and a slogan. This is strictly institutional advertising. The ad is designed to appeal not only to a broad spectrum of people, but also a broad spectrum in terms of where they are in the "motivation pipeline." In other words, assume that from first thinking about buying an expensive home to actually buying it is about an eighteen-month process. If somebody's at the very beginning, you know they're eighteen months out—they won't necessarily respond to the ad directly. Rather, they may go to the website featured because they don't have to "bother" anybody or be bothered. If they are not "captured" at this point, they can be lost.

An institutional ad presents only one message to a potential buyer or seller, so it needs to be a memorable one. If buyers want to find out more about your firm, they have to call somebody, or they can check it out online. The institutional ad might get somebody no matter where they are in the process, or whether they're looking for bay front, ocean front, or Lake Front. This method can reach everybody, but its effects aren't lasting. You're expecting a lot from potential buyers who will likely forget the ad when they turn the page.

Institutional ads work best when done on a frequent and consistent basis. Can you say cash burn?

RESPONSE

I like response advertising because basically no matter where buyers are in the process or the motivation pipeline, and no matter what they're looking for, a properly constructed response ad will pique interest. It provides more than just a glimpse of a particular high-end property with basic information; the ad engages its audience with something of value. It doesn't matter if, as a buyer, I'm looking at the lake, the bay, or the ocean because the ad has just intrigued me with the promise of information I need either now or in the not-too-distant future.

The ad entices readers with a valuable offer of information such as a report. It should tempt them with dramatic titles such as "The Seven Biggest Mistakes Waterfront Buyers Make When Buying Property on Cape Cod" or "The Seven Biggest Pitfalls of Buying Waterfront Property on Cape Cod." It should be inviting, not intimidating. You want readers to believe they need this information so they will call to get that must-have report. Consider providing them with a means to respond that isn't threatening and allows them to avoid talking with a live person, such as a number to leave a voicemail or an e-mail address.

Make sure the voicemail or web page where they leave their contact information states clearly that their privacy will be maintained and that their information will not be sold or given out to others.

THE ONE-TWO-THREE COMBINATION

For the most effective results, blend all three advertising types, or at least combine two out of the three. So anytime you place a property-specific ad you feature the property but also turn it into a response ad by offering a report that gives ad readers inside tips on how to become better prepared buyers or sellers. Again, make the title memorable: "Everything You Need to Know about Buying Waterfront Property on Cape Cod. Leave a voicemail or e-mail for this free report."

When you state "leave a voicemail" or "send an e-mail" for a free report, they know they don't have to talk to anybody. This increases your response rate because it gives them a low-pressure choice of how to reply. The payoff: You're both getting something from the ad.

SET YOUR GOALS THEN YOUR SIGHTS

These three kinds of advertising provide the platform to get your products noticed. But having a goal for what you want your advertising to achieve is paramount to maximizing your advertising resources. Have a purpose, or goal, for each ad, and don't become distracted from it. Most important, don't over-commit resources to doing print ads.

Most real estate ads are a complete sensory assault. I compare them to walking into a large department store at the mall. Racks and piles of clothes and other items are jammed in and piled everywhere. There's probably something you want in the mishmash, but it's too hard to pick through it all.

I prefer to go into a boutique or small shop somewhere. Maybe it doesn't have what I want, but I'm willing to take the time to poke through it because I don't want all those choices. I want it narrowed down to a range of items I'm interested in. I don't want to have to look through things that are crammed together and overflowing.

The same goes for advertising. You need to keep it clean, you need to keep it simple. Less is more.

What are You Looking At?

The most common mistake made in real estate advertising is trying to jam too much information into a small space. Remember, in advertising, less is more. Include more white space with less clutter.

I'm fond of using the phrase "eye bites." How much can your eye absorb in one bite? Consider a For Sale sign. Can your eye take it in with one bite? Too often a company's branding is ineffective because people can't absorb the name in one bite—whether they're reading it in an ad, on a letterhead, in a brochure, or driving by. The more "bites" required to digest your message, the less likely it is to be effective.

The ultimate one-bite logo is IBM. That logo or branding is perfect for your eye to digest in one bite. How many bites do people have to take with their eyes to get your message? If your firm has a long name, come up with a catchy memorable URL that is easy to remember when seen from a moving vehicle. For example, I have always thought of using www.CapeCotton. com as a URL for my market.

My house has a long driveway. When I was creating new signage, I installed the final designs for my company logo and name along the side. I'd drive out in the morning and drive back in the afternoon. Sometimes I would just drive around and around to notice all sorts of signs! I was using my "buyer's eyes" to see which design could be taken in with one eye bite while a person is driving.

Many agents can't resist the temptation to add rider after rider to a simple and effective sign: Waterfront; Dock; New Price: Agent Name, and on and on. But they're defeating the whole purpose. Remember, how many eye bites? Your eye can't take it in if it's too small, too much, or too cluttered.

Agents who like using their name and cell numbers are not going to like this advice. Remember, a passer-by can only see and register so much from a sign. Decide what is important to convey in your signage and resist the temptation to add riders on riders.

Domain names can especially suffer from this. An elaborate multi-word, multi-slash web address is ineffective and even bothersome for its users: www.realestatecompanyx.com/whatever. You simply can't take in a web address that includes at least three bites. Who's going to remember it? Nobody.

BUDGET

An outsized percentage of your overall budget can be devoted to advertising if you're not careful. When asked, I tell agents that they spend 10% of their commission on marketing. A well-run company endeavors to spend between 4% and 6%. But often they're spending 10% or more.

A fairly high percentage of gross commissions within a company goes to the agents. After an off-the-top fee for the franchise or similar costs, a company might be left with only 10% to 24% of the gross commission. You can see the problem if a company spends 10% of the gross commission on ads. In addition, business expenditures besides marketing must be considered.

BUCK SHOT

A fine line exists between overwhelming readers of your ad and interesting them with a variety of options. That's why to get the biggest bang, you need to use a shotgun rather than a rifle. If you place one ad for one house, you're crossing your fingers that everybody likes that one house because otherwise they're not going to call.

Some people put two to twelve houses in an ad to overcome this problem. However, the more houses you put in the ad, the more you dilute it and the harder it is to read. It overwhelms people. So what's the happy medium? Perhaps four to six houses in the ad. That way, you're increasing your chances that at least one will appeal because you're casting a wider net—without overwhelming your readers. The more general your audience, the more houses you feature in an ad.

REEL SITUATIONS OF REAL ESTATE ADVERTISING

As you may have noticed, I love fishing metaphors. They work well in the business of luxury real estate. You want to talk about the big one you landed, not the one that got away.

If you're out on the water with a fishing line off your boat trolling with one kind of lure, you hope the fish will take that lure. But if you add two rods, then two more—some with different lures and others with live bait—you end up with five chances to land something.

However, if you put too many lines off the back of your boat, they will tangle and the fish are likely to "think" what is this mess going by? They have too many options. They can't decide so they don't bite.

The same thing happens to home buyers and sellers reading ads. If they're presented with too many intertwining choices, they don't want to read any *of it. (Luckily, fish have little trouble with real estate ads because they can't read. If they could, we could just troll with one line offering a free report, "The Seven Biggest Dangers to Fish Feeding Near the Surface.")*

The fishing metaphor also applies to wealthy folks because they tend to travel in schools; they stick together.

As an alternative to trolling with multiple fishing lines, park yourself over a school of potential high-end buyers and cast your line with a property-specific ad. This has a better chance of working than a generic ad. You've got one house; you've got one lure. You know the right buyer is down there in the school.

The water is wide and deep. You can either put six lures out, use a generic lure, or park yourself over a school with a specific lure. I prefer the last option.

THE COMPANY YOU KEEP

"You're known by the company you keep" is one line that comes to mind when someone asks me where to place their ads. My answer: "Who are your potential clients and what are they reading?"

You have a thousand publications to choose from. *The Wall Street Journal* is fantastic. *Unique Homes* is great. It's worthwhile to weigh the option of mixing classified and display ads. Ideally, you want your ad to be found within the media luxury real estate owners are reading.

Once, our agency was advertising in a magazine owned by a company that published several magazines. It messed up our ad, and a company rep said the company would give me neither a refund nor a rerun of the ad. As a compromise, the rep said the company would give me a free ad in one of its other publications—a magazine for a major U.S. airline.

My first reaction was less than favorable. ("Are you kidding me?") Well, they gave me the big color ad in the airline magazine and the response was phenomenal. This led us to advertising in airline magazines. At private airports, we found magazines that make their way into private jets—for an exclusive clientele with particular tastes including luxury homes. By chance, I discovered a whole new readership.

The point is to know who your buyers are and what they are reading. You want your ads to be seen in those publications.

GEOGRAPHIC FLEXIBILITY

Buyers in the high end frequently buy homes in close proximity friends and associates. Sometimes, however, they just want to be someplace cool. They don't care where it is as long as it's on the East Coast. Their geographic flexibility works in your favor because these buyers have the means to move wherever they desire.

If you place an ad for a house in an exclusive location, potentially a million people will see it. This high-end geographic flexibility gives you leverage so you have a chance of the ad working no matter where the house is located. The trouble is if you've placed the ad where a million people will see it, it's costing you a fortune. So you want to make sure your ad takes advantage of this geographic flexibility and highlights the unique features of your property. Some ad readers may be looking for specific features such as a deep water dock, a fantastic golf course nearby, or a large tract of waterfront land. In cases where home features are more important to the potential buyer than specific location, you might gain from the geographic flexibility that high-end individuals enjoy.

THE ADVERTISING GIVE AND TAKE

Advertising is a necessary evil. I'm always mindful that it can suck up resources mercilessly. And to educate our sellers that it's the most expensive, least effective thing we can do to sell their house is part of the job of a luxury agent. All the advertising in the world won't sell a property that's not positioned properly in the marketplace.

Print advertising is important, but know why you're doing it so you'll know if it's working. Is it to attract a buyer, or are you trying to keep it in front of the sellers to show you're active? Perhaps you're the owner of the company and want to use it as a recruiting tool. Some ads may be designed to attract agents who might want to work in your company—but they don't effectively sell houses.

Ultimately, it's not the ads but qualified, trained agents who sell houses. However, these agents can't sell unless they have prospects to sell to. People must be drawn into their circles so they can find out what these prospects' needs and desires are and help meet them. This is the purpose of all marketing, including print advertising. Use it wisely.

13

WORD OF MOUSE

THE DANGER OF WRITING THIS CHAPTER IS THAT IT COULD BE obsolete in an hour. You need to find a way to keep up with the warp speed of advances in technology and World Wide Web marketing. This chapter serves as an overview of Internet best practices in the high-end real estate world.

Many people consider me to be a technology guru and totally "up" on everything to do with the Internet. Whenever I join a group, I get stuck on the technology committee. The truth is that while I'm no tech guru, I love technology and I'm an early adopter of new gadgets and software. Sometimes *too* early, expending time and money on something that doesn't always work out.

Some high-end sellers and luxury agents are skeptical about whether multimillion-dollar properties should be listed in the local multiple listing service. With the increasing amount of geographic flexibility among high-end buyers, I believe it's a mistake to omit your local multiple listing service. I've always had the philosophy that in marketing any piece of real estate, no stone should be left unturned.

The web site Realtor.com speaks for itself. Potential buyers from all over recognize this as the largest single source for real estate listings.

As this chapter addresses, MLS and Realtor.com are basically a searchable online form of the old MLS book. To make your high-end listings stand out from the pack, you need to expand them on the Internet.

THREE TYPES OF SITES

We cover three types of web sites in this chapter: agent, company, and property specific. Each of these three has unique characteristics, requirements, and demands. At the same time, they share many common elements.

Agent sites and company sites are virtually the same in terms of function and overall information offered to visitors. The agent site is a smaller version of a company site. Both have listings, neighborhood information, and market data. The main difference is that the agent's site includes less information about the office and more about the agent, and only the agent's personal listings.

For example, at the time of this writing, we have more than 170 properties listed on our local agency's site in addition to those from the MLS. By comparison, an agent may only display his or her own listings, which would be a far smaller number. Whether to go this route or show all properties from your own MLS is a personal business decision. The beauty of an agent site is that it carries less information but that information is more focused on properties that you specialize in than an MLS site. Agent sites can and should have the capability to search your entire MLS.

An agent's site, like a company site, typically features mortgage information, a home valuation form, an agent bio, and testimonials. In most cases, agents have flexibility on who they display as affiliates on their personal web sites. For example, your company's web site may only allow its own lender to be featured with mortgage rates and links.

The consumer benefit to an agent site is simple: less clutter and therefore a lot less information for people to sift through. It's easy for a company or agent site to grow over time to hundreds of pages. No one wants to be distracted by hundreds of pages when all they want is listing information.

Property-specific sites are just that: web sites dedicated to one specific property. Typically, the URL is the property address. These sites will be discussed in detail later in this chapter.

SEARCH ENGINE OPTIMIZATION

The most important thing to know about search engine optimization (SEO) is that the parameters change constantly so constantly discuss SEO issues with your web site administrator.

I talked with Dan Kompass of Webfodder (www.webfodder.com), the company that does my agent site and sites for all types of businesses as well as real estate. This company seems to have a handle on SEO. I frequently see two or three of its clients in the top ten results of any Google search on the industry of its clients.

At the time of this writing, a search for "Cape Cod homes for sale" results in seven sites designed by Webfodder among the top twenty sites.

Dan advises never to let SEO be an afterthought. Successful sites must be initially designed around SEO because it's difficult, inefficient, and costly to add SEO to an existing site. You want to build the site top down, left to right, because that's how engines look through your site.

For every site that Webfodder designs, an SEO document is created that has all the items that a search engine looks for in different parts of your web site.

Dan also advises paying attention to the navigation within the site itself. He suggests naming all the URLs contained within the site with built-in keyword phrases.

For example, let's say you have a page that's called "Agents" with a corresponding navigation button. Instead of a graphic "Agent" button or a mouse over, he suggests creating a text-based button. Style sheets are used to create that "button look" on your web site. Graphic images as navigation buttons offer nothing for search engines to see.

When the button is clicked, the page that comes up should have a name that mirrors the text on the text-based button. Examples include cape-cod-real-estate-agents.htm and chatham-real-estate-agents.htm.

With keyword phrases added to URL strings, you have taken another step to make the search engines find you.

Also be specific in all of your URL and page names. You will be found faster as "Smithville Real Estate" than you will as "Arizona Real Estate." Likewise, "Arizona Real Estate" in your name would make you more visible than just "Real Estate." Be specific everywhere you can. On the World Wide Web, being a big fish in a small pond is a good strategy. In other words, make your name stand out in your field of expertise.

The next concept is inbound links. The more inbound links, you have to your site, the better. For example, webfodder.com has 44,000 inbound links. Any way you search for real estate web sites, you'll find this little web design company on Cape Cod on the first page. You want the same for your luxury real estate web site.

The more links your site has, the higher your score known as "page rank," a 1 to 10 ranking, with 10 being the best. It's how Google rates your web site compared to other web sites of the same type. The more inbound links, the higher the page rank. The higher the page rank, the higher you will show up in the natural searches that is to say, those that are not the result of paid clicks. Many web visitors resist clicking on the obvious pay per click links found on search pages.

You can ask your web provider to start a linking program, or you can hire an outside company to accomplish this. A Google search for linking services will lead to dozens of companies that will submit your site to hundreds of directories. They will follow up with spreadsheets that have live links. You can click on these links to find your web site in a particular directory.

Tags for Your Website

Tags are an important part of your website. Below, you'll see a brief description of the types of tags you need on your website. Understand, however, that a good web designer will be aware of these. Although a book could be written about these tags, this section is intended to give an overview. You can use your desk telephone without knowing how to take it apart and reassemble it. The same goes for your web site.

Resist the temptation to get too detailed in its inner workings. What's important? Knowing what to ask for from your own web designer.

Make sure your site has these important tags:

Title tag: Located at the top of the page in the blue bar above Back and Forward and mostly unnoticed by visitors, this is one of the most important SEO features. Search engines put a lot of weight on this tag, so consider it carefully.

Your site tag might say "Real Estate, Cape Cod homes for sale in Chatham, Barnstable, MA." So you've got real estate for sale, homes for sale, Cape Cod real estate for sale, Cape Cod homes for sale, Chatham homes for sale, Chatham real estate for sale. You wind up with all those keywords in just that one short title tag.

Home tag: Ninety percent of real estate web sites don't use this tag, but it's important. Continuing our example, the home tag might say "Chatham homes for sale." The result? You have more keywords right where the search engines are reading. Remember, search engines read the web site top down, left to right. This tag might be compared to the logo or template text at the very top of a PowerPoint slide.

Header tags: If you were to look at 50 real estate web sites, typically only five of the 50 will have header tags. Header tags are like bullet points on a PowerPoint slide. The name might cause one to think that they are at the top of the page, but in fact they are in the body of the page.

Meta tag: This is the second most important tag on your web site. It is the description that is displayed in the search engines and key-words, and a call to action are very important if used here correctly. For example my own meta tag might look like this:

Waterfront Homes and Luxury Real Estate for sale, Oster-ville…Sotheby's International Realty, Jack Cotton Realtor® – Luxury Village Properties and Waterfront Homes for Sale on Cape Cod Mas-sachusetts, give Jack a call today for more information on Luxury Properties on Cape Cod.

When you do a Google search, the words that come up after the web address of the site that met your criteria are from the Meta tag. These words give a good description of what the site is about and may affect your decision to click on this particular Google result.

Alt tag: This tag, located behind the page graphics and images, should contain more keywords, such as "Cape Cod MLS listings." When you mouse over a photo on a web site that uses Alt tags, you will see text appear that describes the image in SEO-friendly terms. A Chatham photo might have an alt tag that says "Chatham Home For Sale."

H1 Tag: Again, many web sites, real estate or not, leave out these tags. Unwise. Search engines specifically look for H1 tags. This tag is comparable to the Title near the top of a PowerPoint slide.

For example:

H1 Tag: **Real Estate in Chatham**
H2 Tag: **How to find Real Estate in Chatham**
H3 Tag: **Where to find Real Estate in Chatham**

To Log In or Not to Log In

Different schools of thought weigh in on whether visitors to your site should be forced to log in to gain listing information. I don't think you should ever force anybody to log in too early in the search process.

My advice is based on the principle "give before you expect to receive." Sound familiar? You can set up plenty of opportunities to capture names and contact information. For example, have site visitors request more information, request a showing, or e-mail a friend. These require log ins.

Obviously if people sign in, they're serious and they expect someone will contact them because they just gave their name and at least their e-mail address. The beauty is that you've created another visitor action that can be measured.

The back end of your site should be designed so you have a way of collecting, saving, organizing, and contacting logged-in visitors individually and as a group. Good back-end design includes a searchable database function. Talk to your web designer about how to do that.

Keep It Simple

Here are ways to make your overall site layout simple and clean:

- A paragraph that describes the property with the address.
- Professional, properly sized photographs of the property.

126

◆ One feature photo and rows of thumbnails adjacent to it instead of a column of large photos that force the visitor to scroll down the page. When you scroll over the thumbnails, the feature photo changes to the photo you're on.

Real Trends and *1000 Watt Consulting* recently published a study of web sites of the top 500 non-franchise real estate companies in the United States. All 500 sites were exhaustively examined and studied. I highly recommend you go to www.realtrends.com and obtain this report to see examples of the best sites of the 500 that were studied. Keep in mind, these were only company web sites; no agent sites or franchise sites were considered. Nevertheless, you can learn a lot from what these successful sites are doing.

EARLY ADOPTERS

My company, founded in 1974, has been on the cutting edge of technological advancements during these three and a half decades in business. I've always loved the newest technology. Therefore, I could identify with one of the problems the study found with many company web sites. That is, early adopters of an online presence made significant investments back when web sites were extraordinarily expensive to design, update, and maintain. This heavy investment makes some owners and managers reluctant to invest further in their sites to meet the demands of today's buyer.

In our case, I know we had features on top of features cobbled together. Based on consumer feedback, the user's experience did not suffer, but some of the workings were Rube Goldberg-like. We were so in love and comfortable with our site's back end that we didn't want to wipe the slate clean and start over.

From time to time, we did change the look of our site and updated the public appearance; but its back-end functionality and usability didn't change that much, even as new and better functions came along. Also, we were always on the first page of Google searches for our market and we didn't want to jeopardize this. In many cases, however, it's wise to consider starting fresh with an entirely new look, simplified functionality, and a back end that's easy for agents and staff to use.

As with all aspects of high-end real estate, I adhere to the principle of "less is more." As discussed in the advertising chapter, many real estate practitioners have a hard time overcoming the urge to put ten pounds of content into a five-pound bag. This is evidenced over and over in many agent and company web sites. The front page is jammed with endless jpegs, text boxes, banners, and information. Keep it fresh, keep it clean, keep it simple. The fewer buttons the better. Make it pleasing to the eye.

A major criticism contained in the *Real Trends/1000 Watt Consulting* study was the common trend of company web sites having multiple buttons for searching: Quick search, MLS search, Feature Property search, for example. A quick search button leaves the impression that the other search buttons on your page are slow and cumbersome. I suggest having one search button; keep it simple and clean, with all the information that your consumer could want. This applies to agent web sites as well.

If a survey were taken among consumers and agents about what the two groups look for in web sites, you would get diametrically opposed answers to the survey questions. Visitors to real estate web sites want property information, pure and simple. This includes maps, directions, value information, market data (especially sold information), and neighborhood information with links to schools, parks, clubs, and recreation areas. Agents, on the other hand, want lots of photos of themselves with glowing prose about their capabilities, which is basically a Facebook page on steroids.

Remember the acronym WIIFM, "what's in it for me"? The reason consumers come to any web site is to find out what's in it for them.

In my experience, most online consumers want to put off live interaction with an agent for as long as possible. Quite frankly, if they could, I think many potential buyers would conduct the entire process online without ever talking to an agent. Therefore, the more you use your site to educate and inform with relevant content, the greater the likelihood of a consumer "clicking through" to interact with you in person.

FRESHNESS COUNTS

Here's a concept: Make sure the properties listed are actually for sale! In other words, keep your content fresh.

Today, many real estate web sites get direct feeds from MLS so the content is updated automatically. In "the old days" of Internet real estate marketing, we actually had to enter each and every listing into our web sites. Many times, a potential buyer would search the web site of a competing company only to find that the property they were interested in had sold several months before.

With agents and companies making use of blogs, even more chances to miss stale content exist. If you're going to have a blog, make sure it's up to date. Indeed, I'm reluctant to add a blog on my personal site because I'm wary of the commitment to its daily or weekly maintenance.

DON'T SET UP DEAD ENDS

How many times have you been driving down the highway and needed gasoline, a bottle of water, or a cup of coffee? You see the big sign at the next exit promising food, restroom, and fuel services, so you pull off at the exit—but you spot no such services. To make matters worse, you see no signs pointing you in the proper direction to reach the services you're looking for. I'd wager many of us have experienced this frustration on road trips.

These same types of dead ends often occur on real estate web sites. A consumer clicks on a button for "What's My Home Worth," "Local Information," or "Find an Agent," and he or she gets lost in a myriad of clicks. New windows pop open to a point where the original search becomes lost entirely. Conclusion: Eliminate dead ends on your web site.

The Demand for Video

Some agents and companies are now adding video to their sites. If you're unable to do this in a quality manner, I would avoid it. One danger of video marketing for listings consists of providing too much information.

Keep in mind that whether site visitors are searching print ads or the Internet, their main goal is to eliminate possibilities from their consideration. The more information you present, the easier it is for a visitor to your site to eliminate a property. Giving visitors a reason to call or contact you for further information is your goal. That's why you want to strike a balance between giving visitors enough information to want to schedule an appointment and not so much they feel they don't need to see the property.

Also, some people just are not good presenting in front of the camera. I, for example, am more comfortable on radio. As soon as I see a camera, I freeze up, and my eyes dart all over the place, which doesn't make a great impression. You can see others like me on your local cable channel promoting their companies in an awkward, stiff fashion that will turn most viewers off.

A guy doing ads on our local cable channel is an expert in solving IRS tax problems. His ad shows a full-screen close-up of him. The poor fellow is obviously so tense and uncomfortable that this feeling comes right through the TV screen. If I ever needed tax advice, he would be the last person I'd contact.

So if you want to use a video of yourself, I'd advise watching it first. Painful, I know, but necessary.

Two more features you might want to consider on your company or agent web site are language translation and currency conversion, discussed in the following chapter.

Make sure the back end of your web site, whether company or agent, is easy to use and functional. It should provide a way of managing prospects and contacting them either individually or as a group once they have signed up. You also want to receive an alert via e-mail, cell phone call or text, or PDA whenever someone registers on your site so you can give the registrant a speedy response. It's also helpful for your web site to track the features people have been looking at, what properties they've been viewing, and how long and how frequently they view a particular property.

Domain Names

The hard-and-fast rule on choosing domain names is to keep it as simple and memorable as possible. I like property-specific web sites because the address is the domain name. The address of your property is much easier to remember than some arbitrary inventory or MLS number.

As far as your company goes, simplicity is equally significant. If your name has twenty-seven syllables, think of a shorter version or a different name that describes where you are or what you offer to make your domain name more memorable. I wish I'd been quick enough to grab the name www.capecod.com when URLs first came on the scene. That would have a game changer for my real estate business since hundreds of thousands of Google searches for the words "Cape Cod" take place each month. Talk about a prime piece of real estate.

Next in the series of market activities is the selection of web sites you use to feature your high-end listings. You'll include your personal and company web sites, Realtor.com, and your local MLS. In addition, several commercial real estate web sites are available that specialize in luxury properties. They are:

www.luxuryrealestate.com
www.uniquehomes.com
www.luxuryportfolio.com
www.wallstreetjournal.com
www.newyorktimes.com
www.dupontregistry.com
www.iht.com

Your company and personal agent web sites should feature custom search capabilities. I suggest that in addition to the IDX multiple listing search buttons found on nearly all agent and company web sites, you have a search tab for special or exceptional properties on your web site. This tab would access a database of your own listings and can also be programmed to search for properties over a certain price point in your marketplace. Not only are potential buyers looking for this shortcut to special property searches, but if you don't have it, potential sellers will note this unfavorably when they interview you to market their property.

PROPERTY-SPECIFIC WEB SITES

Some readers of this book may recall the old days of real estate when we had the huge MLS books. In a soft market, you needed a forklift to pick it up because it was so heavy. Back then, we got update sheets each week, and we had to spend hours updating our three-ring binders that contained our market's MLS information.

Some old-timers actually miss those days. After all, not only were we the gatekeepers of the information, but we were also the search and matching tool. That means agents would interview a prospective buyer, taking notes on any scrap of paper available, and then match these criteria with listings that met them. We took full charge of the process!

In many ways, not much has changed. Sure, the updates are made on a moment-by-moment basis and buyers can fill in their own criteria on a web form rather than the agent using a scrap of paper. The result, however, is still an MLS form or forms on a computer screen describing individual properties. Depending on how you do your search, you may find a $300,000 home coming up next to a $3,000,000 home. Yes, you'll see a lot more photographs, all in living color, but the information is still on a form.

So MLS remains, in many ways, a search mechanism—an electronic reference book—not a marketing tool. But now clients can match their criteria to the listed properties themselves.

FORMS VERSUS INDIVIDUAL PROPERTY SITES

I've always been averse to using forms. Even after nearly three decades in the business, I have trouble finding information on a form. In areas with more than one MLS, the forms can be dissimilar, resulting in an even greater challenge for a buyer—especially if they're like me.

Some of these issues persist even with a company or personal agent web site: The buyer enters criteria and gets a list of properties with information contained on a form. Lots of photos are included, but it's still a list of forms.

This brings us to the concept of individual property web sites. Several vendors offer templated web sites for individual properties using the property address as the URL. I have become a fan of Platinum Sales Systems (www.youdeserveplatinum.com) in West Lake Hills, Texas, because its services are especially designed for high-end properties. Curt Warner, the company's CEO, and I have discussed numerous benefits of a property-specific web site.

First and foremost is the simple way these sites are promoted with URLs using the property address. Just like our fingerprints are unique, the address of a property is unique. Imagine a newspaper or magazine page full of postage-stamp-sized photos, brief descriptions, and a title, and you'll understand how hard it would be for an interested buyer to find more information on a particular property. Some web sites try to make it "easier" by adding listing numbers, but is that really easier? When you do see advertising for a property, often you'll see a listing number such as 42739-4785. Imagine yourself as a buyer trying to enter that number into a search field on a web site. That is, of course, after you find the web site.

On the other hand, www.127MansionStreet.com is markedly easier to enter. Furthermore, people can enter this address in the search line of any search engine and stand a good chance of finding the property site, especially if the body of the text has been optimized for keywords. Of course, make sure to include a link back to your company and/or agent site from the property-specific site.

This kind of URL also makes it easier to share the site name. Imagine reading a property number to people over the phone; it's much easier to give them the property address for the URL.

From the standpoint of being an effective listing tool, a property-specific web site carries a lot of weight for a seller. All sellers love exposure for their properties; the more the better. Showing them what you have done with an existing listing is compelling, to say the least. Recently, someone who knew one of my sellers commented on the seller's site we had created with a template from Platinum Sales Systems, speculating that I must have spent $10,000 or so to create the site. I can assure you that the investment was nowhere near that, but happily the perceived value is huge.

From the standpoint of an agent, the time savings are worthwhile. For example, our practice has always created a home book for every single listing. The book is comprised of a three-ring binder with a picture of the house on the cover with pages of materials pertaining to the property inside such as deeds, plans, restrictions, neighborhood maps, and amenities. We now put the items that were once included in a home book on the property's web site.

Whereas I used to either fax, copy and mail, or scan and e-mail documents requested by a buyer's agent, now I just refer the agent to www.127MainStreet.com or whatever the property's address URL happens to be. Agents can find every single thing they need to know about that property in one place online, including the closest clubs, restaurants, beaches, and parks.

Curt of Platinum Sales Systems has mentioned that some agents are pre-filling offers to purchase forms with address and title information and having them available on the site as well. What a timesaver for the buyer agent! In some cases, people have even made an offer without an agent because they found the contract on the web site.

Do you see how the property web site becomes a repository of everything you want a potential buyer or agent to see about your listing? You have access to unlimited content including photographs, deeds, restrictions, and neighborhood information. Visitors can bookmark the listing and e-mail the link to friends and family. It provides the potential for "stickiness," the tech word for attracting people back to the site and encouraging them to stay for long periods of time.

Search engine optimization (SEO) can be a challenge but, with any luck, your property-specific web site won't be up that long. You can do certain things such as making sure that all the photo captions and property descriptions use keywords that search engines are likely to find. Also use relevant keywords and terms in the descriptive text, headers, links, and image names. For example, "Osterville Waterfront," "Warren's Cove," "one of the finest waterfront homes for sale in Osterville, MA." Another tip is to use the following structure when naming image files: 109Marquand_Osterville_MA_02655_frontelevation.gif rather than just calling your photos "Image-1" for example.

Linking to other property-specific web sites, a national search site such as www.PlatinumLuxuryListings.com, your personal web site, and corporate web site as well as other syndicated sites will also improve the SEO of your property-specific web site.

Links to community information not only benefit visitors to your site, but also enhance your search engine visibility.

To summarize the difference between a property-specific web site and MLS, an MLS has to appeal to the lowest common denominator of property, agent, and available data. However, when dealing with a high-end luxury property, you don't want to rely on the lowest common denominator vehicle to market the property.

Always Ask "What Does the Client Want?"
The Internet keeps evolving and improving how companies and agents alike get their message to buyers and sellers, challenging their budgets along the way. The important concept to remember in all things Internet is this: *What does the client want?* Ask that question before adding new features as well as evaluating each current feature of your site. Improve those that serve clients in ways they want to be served and eliminate the rest.

14

SOCIAL NETWORKING FOR THE LUXURY AGENT

Social networking may not be the end-all of your real estate business, but it's a fresh, effective way to prospect in the high end.

When thinking about any new marketing technique, especially social networking, your primary question should be "why," not "how." The answers to "Why do we do social networking?" and "Why do we tell people they need to prospect fifty percent of their day?" and "Why do we tell agents to work their sphere of influence?" are all the same: That's where the business comes from. Statistics show that 64% of listings come from people we already know and work with or people they've referred to us.

Good luxury agents prospect and maintain relationships. Some, like Biff and Buffy from Chapter 3, use more traditional methods like golfing or playing tennis with prospects. Yet social media has become a gift in a lot of ways. It's the best technology for staying in touch and listening to our clients in a way that's more cost-effective than mailing and advertising.

Strange and recurring misconceptions in the real estate industry these days surround who's not using social networking. Agents say things like, "I work with a lot of boomers and seniors and, you know, they don't use Facebook." Or, "My clients are really upper end. They don't use social networking." The truth is that upper-end, luxury clients don't own one smart phone; they own two or three.

In fact, the fastest growing segments of our population using social networking are seniors and boomers, according to my friend Matthew Ferrera of www.MathewFerrera.com. We have talked extensively about the advent of social networking and its usefulness to the luxury real estate agent. Much of this chapter comes from our discussions.

Keep in mind, luxury property owners today— regardless of their age demographic—have kids and grandkids, so they're using technology to keep up with and communicate with them. They turn to Twitter to "tweet" their goings-on and use Facebook to stay in touch electronically. No question, the "smart money" people are using smart technology.

We're also finding that high-end buyers are getting younger and younger, with people in their 30s and 40s investing $3 million to $5 million on a summer house. These Gen-Xers are in the beginning of their prime earning years. And so they'll spend $3 million on a summer house or move up into the penthouse apartment in the city. Wherever they go, among their list of desired amenities is high technology connections—broadband, fiber optic, wi-fi, remote control, and so on. They're clearly using these tools to live and communicate.

GUIDELINES FOR YOUR SOCIAL MEDIA

Social networking is a growing phenomenon and can be helpful to business. However, always remember this about social media: You can't put the shaving cream back in the can.

To be effective in social media, you don't have to do anything special; you just have to avoid certain things. For example, let's say you bump into someone from your sphere whom you haven't seen in a while. It could be at a restaurant, a function, or just walking down Main Street. Would you immediately reach into your briefcase and whip out a listing sheet or an invitation to an open house and ask if they want to buy one of your listings? Of course not. You would ask about how they are, what they've been up to, and how things are with the family. You would keep it personal.

The same rule applies to social networking. The value you contribute at this point is enhancing a personal relationship. You connect or reconnect with friends, family, and clients and offer things of value much as you would at a face-to-face meeting during a social event. You might tell a joke or share a news story you found interesting or funny. You remember the guidelines that you learned growing up: Don't talk about politics, sex, or religion. Social networking is just being a person online.

When you meet up with someone in person, you used to bring out photos of children, maybe even your new car or boat. Today, you pull out your iPhone to share the same photos. Now you can use Facebook to share photos of your summer resort market buried in snow or the beach covered in ice.

It's also important to listen. You see, every year research by the National Association of Realtors® indicates that the top 10 reasons people buy or sell a home in luxury or any other market is because of something personal. They got a job, they left a job. They got married, they got unmarried. They're having another kid, or kids are moving out. They're retiring. . . . You get the picture—they're all personal reasons. Well, part of the magic of social media is this: All of your friends are constantly posting information about themselves online. You only have to watch, listen, and learn and you'll be in the right place at the right time.

So when your friend, whose last kid is graduating from college, posts, "We're so excited that Johnny's graduating from college in two months," you think to yourself, "Hey, they might be in the market for some real estate services." The parents might now have money left over to buy their luxury vacation home, or they might want to upscale, downscale, or relocate. Read between the lines and you can discover many possibilities through social networking.

KEEP IT FRESH
To paraphrase Woody Allen, if you want to be successful in your career, you need to show up. Assuming you have a social networking presence, how do you keep it up to date? How much time is spent on this effort hourly, daily, or weekly?

Think about your daily business routine. In the morning, you prob-ably get a cup of coffee, check e-mail, the MLS hot sheet. Then you follow up with existing clients and respond to new web-based cli-ent leads. Let's add checking in on and updating, as needed, your Facebook, LinkedIn, and other online venues. Don't feel you must have an account with every online venue; it's better to "go deep" with one or two than "go wide" with more than you can possibly handle. Quality over quantity.

ONLINE SOCIAL NETWORKING VENUES

Twitter (twitter.com) is probably the hardest social media site to master because of the limited amount of text you can post. Think of Twitter as kind of an announcement service—your PR purveyor. Announce short pieces of information, and watch for and respond to other people's announcements.

Keep it simple by linking your Twitter account to your Facebook and/or LinkedIn pages. When you update them, Twitter automatically "tweets" to anyone who follows you on Twitter with their computer or smart phone. But because you're limited to 140 characters, don't spend a lot of time constructing short, clever sentences. Instead, go to Facebook or a blog and post something new, interesting, and valu-able. Twitter will pick it up, cut it off at 140 characters, and send out a tweet automatically. These tweets can include a hyperlink that enables followers to click and follow the link to the full posting—whether it's an update on another social network, a link to a blog posting, or any other website, video, or Internet content item.

LinkedIn (linkedin.com) is fantastically useful for high-level busi-ness social networking. The major difference between LinkedIn and Facebook is the difference between a cocktail party where you have to wear a tuxedo and a backyard barbecue where you can show up in shorts and sandals. LinkedIn provides a more professional level of interaction. Your profile is your professional résumé of skills and professional accomplishments. This allows you to interact at a purely business level. Don't talk about your vacation; don't post pictures of your kids and pets; and don't make comments intended to be funny.

Use it as an online business after hours. LinkedIn lets people see you professionally.

The Recommendations function in LinkedIn is a total winner because, unlike other testimonials, a written recommendation from one of your past clients can be quickly verified. A future client can read one of your recommendations, click over, and send a message like, "Hi, I'm thinking of working with Jack. I saw your recommendation. Would you mind if I asked a few questions?"

This method helps connect with high net worth individuals because they tend to be skeptical of marketing claims and traditional printed testimonials. LinkedIn turns this totally upside down by making recommendations transparent and verifiable. What could be better for a potential client?

What's more, LinkedIn generates traffic. It allows you to link your blog (if you have one) to your LinkedIn profile. Each time you write a blog entry, it shows up automatically on LinkedIn and alerts all your connections. This drives traffic to your blog. Not only is this service free but it lets you announce your activities to people who've indicated they want to hear from you.

LinkedIn features groups that let you interact with people based on common interest. For example, you can link with real estate groups such as the National Association of Realtors® or CRS or your own company or franchise group, which is a good way to learn from others. You can also search for a group on sailing, horseback riding, finance and investing, antique buying—whatever your interest may be. Through LinkedIn, the potential to meet many luxury clients is incredible.

ActiveRain Real Estate Community (ActiveRain.com) is an online community that falls into a different category than LinkedIn. Your ActiveRain presence is built around a blog, affording an efficient and free way to communicate with the public. Although designed to communicate to your public through a blog, ActiveRain generates a lot of Realtor® to Realtor® communication. In addition, you create networks of other Realtors®, exchanging ideas on each other's blogs and postings. The downside is that it's easy to get caught up in multiple real estate conversations. Discussions about who's right and who's wrong about lockboxes, agency issues, Realtor.com, and the use of digital cameras can eat up a lot of valuable time.

If you blog to the public through ActiveRain, you can obtain excellent search engine exposure. With thousands of people on ActiveRain, search engines pay a lot of attention to it, making it a good way to be found.

Facebook (facebook.com) has become the clear leader in social networking—a position once held by MySpace. However, MySpace's demographic is much, much younger, catering to the 13-to-25-year-old age bracket. If you're looking to interact with luxury clients, you're apt to have more success on Facebook than MySpace.

Think of Facebook as the equivalent of your high school yearbook online. You can easily reconnect and catch up with old friends, family members, and people you haven't heard from in the town you grew up in. I used to think Facebook was a waste of time until I received a friend request from a past client who owns a multimillion-dollar home in my market. So I asked, "Who else is on Facebook?" I recalled the days many years ago when I drove my older kids and their friends from place to place. I used to drive slowly because I loved to hear them talk among themselves about everything. A great way to stay up to date with what was going on in their lives.

Today, Facebook supplements those chauffeur duties as an effective way to keep up with who your kids are talking to and what they're saying. Like others, people of means are clued in to social networking, if for no other reason than wanting to keep up with their children.

On Facebook, it might be appropriate to have funny pictures of yourself, tell amusing stories, and post humorous YouTube videos. Some people play online computer games and use gifting applications. Think of Facebook as the country fair, where you bump into people, interact with them, and always see something new. What a relaxed way to prospect.

High-end prospecting tools—phone calls, e-mail templates, newsletters—all can be formal, stilted, structured, and dull. With Facebook, you can talk to people in a lighthearted way.

At the time of this writing, more than 400 million people are using Facebook. I suggest you make a posting here and note the speed with which you receive replies. This is where I post snowy photos of Cape Cod or the thermometer at our ski condo reading 20 below zero.

YouTube (youtube.com) is considered an input tool, unlike Twitter and Facebook, which are output tools. If you post something on Facebook or Twitter, it gets announced to the world (or at least to those connected with you on those venues). YouTube works the opposite way because postings aren't announced. However, you can upload useful videos and link them to your Facebook group to let that sphere of influence know about it. Then they're able to watch that video.

You can use YouTube to provide valuable information to your followers. Create videos on the local property tax situation or features of your market that establish you as an expert and help with your SEO if it's on your web site. You could also create short videos featuring your listings. Like me, you may believe you have a face for radio and don't want to do video. If that's the case, get over it. Do it more and you'll get over it and get better. Trust me; I am working on this myself as I am extremely uncomfortable with video. At the same time, if I want to establish myself as an expert and make the best use of video, I will have to get comfortable. Think back to our chapter on public speaking. I used to get physically ill before every talk. Now I just have a racing heartbeat, shallow breath, and cold sweats. We all progress when we move out of our comfort zone. "Just Do It" as the saying goes.

In addition to your own videos, you can share other people's videos. (Caution: be sure the content is appropriate. Sometimes what I think is funny you might find offensive.)

This free tool provides massive traffic that can certainly give your listings exposure. Take the extra step and post your videos regularly. In addition to Facebook, there are other sites listed near the end of this chapter that will post short videos automatically to multiple Facebook-like sites.

Posting links to videos does occur in LinkedIn, but more rarely than in Facebook. On LinkedIn, the audience expects recommended links to *anything* to be high-quality, robust content. Posting a link to your blog article talking about the local market—which also features a video—is likely more attractive to those who use LinkedIn. On Facebook, watching a video of any quality—homegrown or professionally shot—is part of the laid-back culture of the network. As for posting on YouTube, you simply post the video and anyone who has "subscribed" to your account will receive an email alert that you have added new content.

QUANTITY VS. QUALITY

When it comes to the number of social networking venues you're active in, depth is greater than width, as previously mentioned. This concept applies to the number of contacts you have within your Facebook and Twitter sites. Sometimes I get Twitter or Facebook envy when I see agents with 4,000 friends. But being successful in real estate isn't about volume; it's about working a specific sphere of influence that's tightly networked. These interconnections can help you generate a sufficient amount of revenue every year. So don't think you have to accept every invitation to be a friend with someone; be selective.

After all, it would be hard to do anything meaningful with thousands of friends. You could post something that half of them like and perhaps insults or doesn't interest the other half. Remember emphasizing the need to listen to people in our sphere? How can you listen to 4,000 people?

BUILD YOUR NETWORK

If you have a sphere of influence database, you're well on your way to building your friends and contact base within the social networking area. To build your friends group on Facebook, for instance, search for each person from your sphere of influence list and send each one a friend request.

It's not hard. After you build a profile in Facebook or LinkedIn, both automatically begin finding and suggesting people you might know. When you add your graduating class from your college or high school, you'll get a message that says, "Do you know these people?" You just click to connect, and the system facilitates the connection process instantly.

From your business, take the last 75 transactions and list all parties to the transaction including, of course, the buyer and seller. Add them to your Facebook under a specific category. After you add your family and friends, you would categorize your business connections, too. Why? You don't want all your Facebook connections to see the same things. For example, I can post a photo of me at the beach to friends, but I need a category called "business acquaintances" who won't have access to that photo. However, I might want them to see an article from *The Wall Street Journal* that relates to real estate.

Think about the power of the personal introduction. If I become friends with someone, I might think Joe should know Connie. I click on Connie's page and recommend her to Joe. When Connie receives a message that says Jack thinks Joe should know Connie, I have helped facilitate a connection. It could be someone I've never met before, but the beauty of a third-party introduction can be magic. It's like being at a cocktail party and having someone I know walk over to me and say, "Hey, I want you to come meet someone" and I get an introduction.

Of course, you would never bring two people together at a cocktail party and say, "Connie, Joe wants to be your friend." The same holds true with social networking. When making a friend request or referral, take the time to write a little introduction and explain why you think the connection would be beneficial for both parties. Anything less is just not polite.

Today, services are available to help you create and update your social networking pages; just be careful not to wind up with an engineered or contrived presence online. If your postings come from you, that should be obvious. Postings coming from a service or auto-bot are also obvious, but in a negative way. People pick up on this "engineering" and sense the insincerity of your social networking presence.

If you're new to social networking, take it slow at first. Someone might say something or post something with which you disagree. Just as with e-mail, resist the temptation to respond quickly. Disagree in your mind first; you don't have to disagree online. With online written comments, you don't have the benefit of inflections and body language so chances of being misunderstood are multiplied.

MORE SOCIAL MARKETING TIPS

Recently, I learned several things you can do to pick up the pace and stay ahead of your competition in the social networking arena from my friend Ed Primeau of www.VideoProductionPrimeau.com. Try them out!

1. ***Create a marketing video and get it seen.*** Step outside the social media box and post your video on as many video delivery web sites and communities as possible. More than 50 sites allow you free visibility by uploading your video to their community, thus increasing your viewership. Rather than advertising specific properties, create short three-minute videos using catchy search engine friendly titles. Remember the headlines we created in Chapter 4? These are also perfect titles for your videos. You can take the content from one of your reports and your web address should be at the bottom of the screen through the entire movie A few you may not have thought of include:

   Buzznet
   Esnips
   Flixya
   Metacafe
   Motionbox
   VideoWebTown
   Vimeo

   Ed told me to think of this analogy: If you had one TV in an airport where thousands of people traveled every day, more than likely a lot of people would see the programming. However, if you had dozens of TVs in the same airport, the numbers of viewers would dramatically increase in proportion to the number of TVs. The same holds true for the Internet. The more visibility you have, the more viewers you will have and the more inquiries you will receive.

2. ***Use social media to educate and inform your market.*** Many people use social media for promotion but neglect to provide value and content. Give your followers, family, and friends something to talk about. Before you invite us to another "fan club," ask the questions "So what? Who cares?"

Your postings should always meet at least one of the following criteria:

◆ Gain respect and cement your image as an expert.

◆ Provide a benefit to your friends, even if it's to just make them smile.

◆ Provide information of value.

In understanding social media, the *how* is easy; knowing *why* you're there isn't as obvious. Face it. Social media won't make you successful if you're not good at being a real estate agent in the first place. Rather, social media augments your prospecting activities; it won't replace them. You still have legwork to do, even if social networking serves as a communications backbone for your clients.

If you employ the tips and techniques outlined in this chapter, you'll be off to a great start using social media to enhance your marketing. Don't forget, though, to break away from your computer and talk to people, either face-to-face or on the telephone. Social networking is new, fun, and ever-changing. It is also a ruthless thief of your time. Keep it in perspective.

15

OPEN HOUSES

"WHAT? ARE YOU KIDDING ME?"

That's the initial reaction many people have when I talk about doing an open house for an ultra-expensive property.

No, I'm not kidding about hosting open houses, even in expensive estate properties. Remember, many times the buyer is a friend, relative, or associate of someone in the area. What better way to get people nearby into the home for sale than hosting an open house?

Agents are often tempted to hold spur-of-the-moment open houses to fill voids in their schedules. This doesn't work in the high-end market. Aside from deciding which type of open house to plan, preparation is critical to making your event successful.

CATEGORIES OF OPEN HOUSES

You can opt for any one of several types of open houses. You can:

- Invite people either by invitation only or opening the estate to the public.
- Have broker-only open houses for selected agents across your area who are known for listing and selling in the high-end category.

◈ Participate in your local MLS listing tour, held weekly in most markets.

◈ Be part of open house events staged for charity.

THE NUTS AND BOLTS

Above and beyond the type of open house, careful planning is required to protect the property. For example, long narrow driveways can pose a problem when an impatient visitor is blocked by cars in front. I have actually seen people drive their cars across lawns in situations like this. Not good. You may need to arrange for valet parking with certain properties or at least assign someone to direct and control the parking during the hours of the open house.

Valuable items need to be either put away and/or inventoried (at the very least). At one house I went to, on a living room table was displayed a small decorative item encrusted with rubies, diamonds, and other precious gems. This item would fit neatly in the palm of a hand or scarcely create a small bulge in a pocket or purse. I can only imagine its value! Make sure valuables cannot be seen by anyone coming through.

Many people believe that any open house involving agents needs to have food. No one likes a free lunch more than I do, but I'm not convinced providing food is necessary during a high-end open house. First of all, what about spills on expensive furnishings or floor coverings? That could be a nightmare.

Instead, seek ways to attract people other than with food. Of course, highlight the unique nature of the property itself. Anticipate that your high-end listing has a strong enough draw that agents will want to see it with particular clients in mind. If you believe your open house needs an extra boost, offer certificates for local restaurants or upcoming events—and advertise them.

No matter which category of open house you choose, yours won't be successful if you conduct it in an impulsive manner. Any open house for a high-end property should be carefully planned in advance so nothing is left to chance.

"By Invitation" Open House

I consider by-invitation-only open houses the most effective means of creating traffic for a high-end listing.

Again, plan well. Invitations must be designed, mailing lists developed, and time allowed for them to be produced, sent, and responded to. For broker open houses and MLS tours, we commonly confirm attendance of invited agents with telephone calls and e-mails the day of the event. It's well worth the time spent.

Begin this process by having a graphic designer create an open house invitation template that can be used to assure the continuity in the "look" of your marketing.

If it's not a broker-only event, send the invitations to neighbors of the property as well as those in similar high-end areas. Inviting people from surrounding properties using addresses gained from tax rolls can be especially effective.

Also invite current buyers on your agency roster and people in your sphere of influence. Remember, people of means like to be around others like themselves.

I have often been skeptical about inviting neighbors to open houses, but I've come around. Why? Because time and again, the response to these events has been overwhelming. We recently had two high-end oceanfront homes open one afternoon. The attendance of neighbors both surprised and overwhelmed us. Even though we provided light refreshments of wine, cheese, and crackers, we learned that the properties themselves brought out the people, not the food and drink.

You'll find that a burning curiosity about the property motivates many visitors to come to your high-end open house. At the same time, they fear being added to a database and hounded endlessly into buying this particular house, so their curiosity must be strong enough to "burn through" their feelings of reluctance. A series of well-planned questions can erase these concerns of your open house visitor.

Questions to Ask During the Open House

After greeting visitors, you can ask questions such as: "What brought you to this open house? Was it the mailing, or advertisement, the Internet or word of mouth?" My next question is always, "Would you like me to show you the home or would you prefer to see it on your own?" If you watch carefully, you will see a wave of relief wash over their faces when you give them an opportunity to walk through the property on their own. This immediately disarms and relaxes them. They sense that you aren't trying to pressure them to buy during every moment of their visit. Typical questions after that include: "Are you looking for yourself or for friends? How long have you been looking? What would you do if you found the ideal property?" And don't forget to ask if they're currently working with another agent.

When the visitors are working with another agent, after I show them the property, I immediately follow with a courtesy call to their agent saying their client is "on the loose." This is a rare courtesy to the agent working with this prospect that will set you apart from your peers.

Be sure to put out a guestbook and ask people to sign in so you collect their names and contact information. Again, expect visitors to be reluctant to provide this information. Therefore, if you give before you expect to receive by offering something of value, you will find it easier to get this information. For example, we keep a copy of our high-end real estate magazine on hand and ask visitors if they'd like a complimentary subscription. To fulfill this desire, we need their name and contact information.

You may have other resources available such as one of your reports with the snappy Cosmopolitan magazine-like headline or other items of interest that could be sent to the visitor after the open house. All of this requires collecting their contact information. It's a powerful way to build your database and sphere of influence with qualified individuals.

AGENT TOURS
Schedule a tour of your luxury listing with fellow agents from your office or company as soon as possible. Agents are in a better position to describe a property to potential buyer clients once they've viewed it in person. And, as discussed in Chapter 8 on pricing, having your office agents tour the property and offer their pricing opinions helps you solidify the correct offering price for your luxury listing.

Just as some agents and sellers are reluctant to put a high-end property in the MLS, often they're even more skittish about having an entire multiple listing tour visit their property on tour day.

I have cringed at times when a large MLS tour arrives to see a special property, creating traffic jams in small lanes and private drives. I have looked on in horror as people have taken shortcuts across lawns or walked through a multimillion-dollar home holding a cup of coffee or smoking a cigarette.

Because larger than normal groups of agents are likely to turn out for an MLS tour of a special high-end listing, tight organization and planning are especially critical. Enlist help from fellow agents in your office, hand out maps delineating parking areas, and give special instructions to prevent bottlenecks that could result in impatient visitors driving over landscaped yards. Consider having them park on the main road and bringing them back and forth to the main residence in golf carts or other conveyances.

An alternative to the MLS tour is a private invitation-only tour for agents who are likely to have buyers in your property's price range. This way, you have more control over the number of people who attend. It also gives you the opportunity to invite agents from other high-end markets who would not typically come on a local MLS tour. You can entice attendance with drawings, wine and cheese refreshments, and other offerings. In fact, local vendors are often more than happy to sponsor an open house that gets them in front of this group of agents.

Some high-end real estate sellers take privacy to great lengths by *suppressing* visits from local real estate agents. These folks don't even want the neighbors to know that the property is for sale. My experience is that neighbors will find out sooner or later. If you don't keep them in the communication loop, you run the risk of having misinformation about your listing disseminated in the marketplace. So be open about your listing.

Conducting neighborhood open houses have been successful for us because people of means often host social gatherings at their properties. At these events, they have the potential to "captivate" those visiting this area for the first time. Often the phrase is uttered,

"This place is fantastic. Gosh, if anything comes on the market in this area, be sure to let me know."

Studying high-end sales in a market such as Cape Cod tells me a high percentage of expensive homes are being sold to friends, relatives, or associates of people already in the neighborhood. This occurs to a higher degree in luxury markets than in normal ones because "people of means" like to be with and among people they know and can relate with.

In many markets today, old money rules because it seems to be somewhat insulated from the gyrations of the economy. This is true because old money is most often held in safe liquid investments like bonds.

KNOW THE LAY OF THE LAND
Beyond hiding the silver and looking for traffic bottlenecks within the neighborhood and property, walk through the home like a buyer and think of every question he or she might ask: "Who was the builder? When was it built? Is there any noteworthy designer responsible for the plan? What improvements, additions, or even deletions have been made over the years?"

We have sold homes that have had entire wings removed and others that have included additions larger than the original home. Along our shorefront, some homes were moved closer to the water and others farther away from it. Sometimes the same dwelling has been moved back and forth several times. You need to know these things, especially because your visiting neighbors will know. It's never good to host an open house in which visitors might know more about the property and area than you do!

Additional questions include: "Has the property ever been featured in any media? Why is the property on the market?"

And be sure to ask *yourself*, "What would the current owners like me to disclose about themselves and their residency here?"

We currently have a property for sale with scores of video cameras ringing the residence. These cameras have both infrared and LED light rings around the lenses for nighttime use. Buyers can't help but notice them, even though some are hidden in birdhouses, hedges, and stone walls. Naturally, they want to know the owners' "story." So you must develop a story—a sales-oriented tale—with your sellers so that visitors' curiosities can be reasonably satisfied. If questions linger unanswered, potential buyers can get totally distracted from evaluating the residence itself. So take time to agree with your sellers what you can and cannot disclose to lookers. Nail down their "story" and tell it consistently at all your open houses and showings.

Lastly, practice showing the property. Bring a fellow agent, a family member, or if necessary, your dog. We are in the only profession in which practice is not part of the program. Pilots practice with simulators and doctors practice on dead people, yet real estate agents want to "operate" on a "live one" right away.

Know where the surprises and good views are; also point out the stained moldings, trim, and other details. You may not get a lot of visitors so don't wait to practice on the few who do come. Be ready!

SPECIAL EVENTS

You can also design and host a special value-added event around a charity and invite high-end individuals from outside your geographic area.

For example, you might team up with the local jewelry store to do an amazing display of high-end estate jewelry at your listed property. We once teamed up with an auction house that wanted to draw attention to the sale of antique golf equipment. This event was eagerly attended by people of means.

Because they're known for being generous with their time and funds, these people are constantly invited to charity events. A typical charity event at your listed property features a cocktail reception, silent and live auction, and dinner. You could add appeal by contacting a local celebrity who's willing to come and sign autographs or sell and sign their books during the event.

SHOW HOUSES

Creating "show houses," either one or a series of them, is a great way to raise money for a local charity and create visibility for you.

One successful plan is to have a high-end property set aside for a charity show house. You'd have each room of the residence decorated by a renowned local decorator. People connected with the charity then sell tickets to tour the house during a one- or two-week period. You gain a lot of exposure by offering your listed property, helping staff the tour, and having your placard and cards around—all in exchange for supplying a residence people want to tour.

What's the downside? This type of event ties up the property while preparing the show house and during the showing hours. You'd have to select a property that's likely to be vacant for several months.

In addition, the property's owner could be required to cover certain infrastructure repairs. At the conclusion of the show, the owner often has the opportunity to purchase accessory items that will move with them, but the paint and wallpaper, of course, remain.

We have had different show house charity events over the years in which the owners were exuberant about having direction to renovate their houses. They committed vast funds to infrastructure improvements, which made the event an even greater success. Results included sales of the show house as well as building new relationships and cementing existing ones with potential clients.

A different but equally effective way to help a local charity is to put together a series of four or five houses (preferably all your listings) that have spectacular gardens, kitchens, or vistas. The charity picks a theme such as a kitchen tour, garden tour, or "homes with a great view" tour. The local charity enthusiastically supplies the personnel to organize, promote, and staff the event. The upside for the charity is enormous; and so is the potential exposure for you, both in terms of your support of the charity and in the numbers of qualified people who will view your homes. Remember, a high percentage of those invited should come from your active listings. Here are some themes you might consider:

Kitchen tour
Garden tour
Library tour
General house tour
Cool garage tour

You can make these tours fun as well as being good for the community, informative for your clients, and of course, a creative way to gain exposure for you.

AFFILIATE MARKETING PARTNERS

You can build traffic for your open house by partnering with affiliate marketing partners. Chapter 10 gives you a wealth of ideas of how to work in affiliation with others for a mutual benefit.

For example, if you can promote your invitational open house by stating that high-end estate jewelry or antique golf equipment will be on hand—perhaps even having an expert available to evaluate antiques—you've created value that likely will lead to a large turnout. You also gain the opportunity to market to the spheres of influence of your affiliates as well as those affiliate marketing partners who offer these services.

You get the idea; be creative. Done properly, open houses can be an extremely effective means of marketing your high-end listing.

16

"DEMONSTRATING" THE PROPERTY BY LAND, SEA, OR AIR

YOU CAN MAKE HIGH-END REAL ESTATE EVEN MORE FUN BY THINK- ing outside the box in how you demonstrate your listings. I use the word "demonstrate" because it reflects involving the buyer in the property rather than merely showing rooms in a house.

So instead of driving up to a ski condo, meet at or bring your client to the base lodge and ski into a luxury slope-side residence. This way, you're not just showing the property, you're clearly demonstrating an advantage of this property.

Similarly, meeting buyers at a local marina and taking them to the property via boat is another way of "demonstrating" the prop- erty rather than just showing it. You accentuate what the property offers and facilitate how they might envision themselves living there. They can fantasize what this estate provides even visiting it for the first time.

Just like using the charity auction certificates discussed in Chapter 18, you can enlist helicopters, hot air balloons, woody beach station wagons, antique fire trucks, or boats for demonstrating your property. Above all, make it fun.

I can tell you that when I'm seen out on the water with jacket and tie and clients on board, it raises eyebrows and causes discussion among the people in my marketplace. ("There's Jack showing property with his boat," they're saying.) Yes, you *want* to be the topic of conversation in a good way. Demonstrating property in fun, unusual ways can make this happen.

RIDE BICYCLES TO DEMONSTRATE

During 2009, gasoline prices declined somewhat. Nevertheless, the need to conserve and do one's part to save energy and protect the planet has never been more important. In many markets, real estate companies in suitable locations are maintaining small fleets of cruiser-type bicycles for showing individual homes to potential buyers and giving overviews of market areas. If I were the owner of a real estate company, I would have had bikes out front of our office during the spike in gasoline prices we endured two years ago. Guess what? Those prices will be returning soon. A great way to attract positive press.

I can assure you that showing homes by bicycle is also happening in the high-end luxury market. Why? Because it's different, it's fun, it's topical, it's exciting, and it sets you apart. Think outside the box. Don't just show your properties; *demonstrate* them!

YOUR EYES—AND OPINIONS—DON'T MATTER

Whether you choose to show it by land, sea, or air, keep in mind that during the property inspection, only two eyes matter—those of your buyer. In showing luxury property for that buyer, step outside yourself and refrain from using your own value system during the property inspection. This sounds complicated and probably is. But the best way to adhere to this practice is to *just keep quiet* during the showings.

For example, you may think the home's decorating is horrific or the layout horrendous, but the buyer might love it (or vice versa). To see the property through the buyer's eyes, refrain from excess narration and carefully study his or her reactions to its features.

Remember that "patter" matters. If you do speak, think about your words carefully. It helps to know about your client before you do, although that's difficult if a co-broker is doing the showing and you're meeting the prospective buyer for the first time.

CHAPTER SIXTEEN

I have overheard showing agents talk about the advantages of particular properties for raising children to a couple who has none, can't have any, has lost one, or will never have any. Don't assume *anything*. In fact, if there's one lesson I've learned over and over again in business, it's that: *Don't assume anything.*

Keep your comments general and—let me emphasize again—keep quiet during the showings.

I usually begin a showing by telling the client, "I'll let you explore the property and I'm willing to answer any questions you may have." It's like saying, "There are certain things I could point out, but I'll keep quiet and allow you to enjoy this property in your own way."

It helps that I'm a quiet person naturally, but if you aren't, be sure to curb your tendency to talk as you let them explore. Focus on watching carefully for buying signals.

As in any price range, different buyers have different reactions, although I believe people's response to a property that "speaks" to them is universal. That's when clients themselves grow quiet and contemplative, then end the showing quickly by saying, "Let's write this up."

Preview the Property—Always

Before demonstrating a high-end property to prospective buyers, always preview the property before the actual showing. Look for surprises like secret panels opening to hidden rooms and determine which areas (like dark, narrow hallways) might need extra lighting during showings.

Because it's unlikely you'll show dozens of high-end properties to a particular buyer, the task of previewing each one shouldn't be too daunting.

Chapter 9 includes a checklist of items for look for. In that chapter, I mentioned showing a property to a potential buyer in the $1 million to $2 million price range. From previewing it, I knew it featured large palladium-style windows opposite the foyer. The view was filled with shimmering light from the sun dancing off the water. But when my client and I arrived for the showing and the showing broker opened the door, I saw that the shades of this huge window were drawn shut.

Being greeted with that shiny water view would have been so much more dramatic! So I dashed across the room and pulled open the shades, but I knew we'd missed the opportunity to make a fabulous first impression. What's the lesson? If necessary, take charge during a showing and don't leave opportunities like that to chance.

No Surprises Allowed

When buyers are coming with their own agent to view a property I've listed, I always arrive 15 to 20 minutes early and here's why. During the listing appointment, I gave my sellers a list of things to be done before every showing. But in a seasonal resort market, the sellers are frequently away from the property, so it's up to me to execute that list.

This is especially important if your showing happens after a recent weather event or no one has been to the property in a while. Always check for broken windows, dead birds lying on the deck from crashing into a sliding glass door, or similar horrors that can disrupt a showing.

One agent was surprised to find the owner of the home sitting in the family room chair. When she had called to set up an appointment with the seller, no one answered the phone so she thought it was okay to come by. It turns out the owner in the chair had left this world. Imagine if the buyer had arrived at the same time as the agent! You never know when you might have to prevent an unfortunate encounter like this!

17

WORLD WIDE
WEALTH

You could write volumes on marketing to international buyers because, the last time I checked, 196 countries graced this world. You could try to learn customs and traditions of all the people in these countries until you go insane, or you could take a more reasonable tack and see what countries are already represented in your market, then learn about them.

In my home market on Cape Cod, for instance, I've noticed German, Russian, and English populations among the local luxury real estate purchasers. So I can use these three countries as jumping-off points for generating my international marketing plans.

I suggest investigating countries represented in high-end sales; they're definitely among the cultures you want to zero in on—the ones who are visiting or prospecting your area. My tack is to look locally, then work globally.

Set Their Sights on Your Sites

To say "the world is becoming a global community more each day" is a cliché. But think what's happening that enables our global community to grow. For one, it's the ubiquity of the World Wide Web that allows a company to connect with visitors beyond borders and share information about luxury listings with them. You can tap into myriad ways to enhance web sites to interact with visitors and showcase premier properties. (See Chapter 13 for more about using the Internet creatively in your marketing.)

Being on the Internet is the best way to attract international buyers because that's how they find what they're searching for. Following are three things you can do consistently that will help.

1. *Make sure your web sites are tagged with proper keywords to attract an international audience.* Say you wanted to target a European clientele who vacations on Cape Cod and who might be prospective purchasers there. You could create a new page on your website with information geared to that type of buyer. It might feature the difference between the Euro and the U.S. dollar and/or rules and regulations pertaining to buying real estate in the U.S. You could include information on any special taxes, fees, or procedures they would want to know about. This page could be optimized for SEO with a title tag of "Buying real estate in the U.S., what you need to know, ask Jack Cotton." However, the keywords you use today may soon be obsolete so it behooves you to have your Internet team constantly update your web site tags.

2. *On your web site and in your ads, include a currency converter to list prices in both Euros and U.S. dollars.* Be sure to use a date disclaimer because the currency conversion fluctuates hourly. It should state something like "accurate as of _____ (a specific date)" to avoid liability issues. Don't neglect including this to accommodate sales to foreign buyers or they'll quickly click over to a competitor's site.

3. *Use language converters on your web site to increase the value of your marketing by giving people an option of using a language they understand.* This clearly shows that you're active internationally. Folks in their home countries browse the Internet in their own language. Because you're dealing with visitors from all over the world, give them a choice of

English, French, German, or whatever. Find out about Google's translation tool to make the job of translating easier.

I love bicycles, especially Italian bikes. When I visit Colnago.com to look for the company's limited-edition Bike of the Year, I'm required to select my preferred language before I can read information on this site. I think it's cool. Adding this feature to your web site can be cool, too!

Here's a bonus: Say I'm going to list your house and I set up a listing appointment. Before I get there, you check out my web site to see how I present my services. You see that you have to select a language before you can read anything on the site. You think, "Wow, this agent must reach a lot of people around the world and has a strong international presence or he wouldn't do this." Perception is reality; offering a language choice creates the perception you want when marketing internationally.

Geographic Flexibility

International buyers have more geographic flexibility than typical American buyers because they have less of a stake in the area. The people who have the greatest geographic flexibility are those who don't have friends or family (essentially a "people connection") in the area they're researching. When you have a people connection in the area, you only look in that area; it's human nature.

Occasionally, a potential buyer says, "Well, I'm looking for something on the water with a dock and a beach, and I'm thinking somewhere between Maine and Delaware." You'd be wise to respond by saying, "Well, within that geographic range, you should really be looking at Cape Cod (or whatever your home area is) because…" Turn a general inquiry into a specific response.

MEDIA WITH A TWIST

It's easy to understand where and why the medium of print still has its place. International business professionals from parts far and wide read the various editions of *The Wall Street Journal, International Herald Tribune,* or *Financial Times*. It's another way to reflect the company you keep.

At the same time, I think that whether you're an international person or a local person thinking of buying real estate in a particular area, you still read local media to get the "inside" track on what's going on. Far-off exotic publications can be great, but don't overlook the importance of inserting international appeal into your local marketing.

If Germans are interested in Miami, chances are they can find an ad for Miami real estate in a local German paper. But typical buyers tend to have a lingering fear that reading only local media leads them to miss something, so they're compelled to broaden their search. They read the Miami, the Cape Cod, or the Beverly Hills paper because of this fear. Although this happens in any price range, it's especially true for high-end properties.

Sellers always ask about the places I plan to advertise. I respond by saying something to the effect of: "Mr. and Mrs. Seller, you may pick up a buyer in a foreign publication, but buyers who are serious about Cape Cod will research Cape Cod media because they're afraid they're going to miss something. They can access all of these newspapers on the Internet these days."

That said, be careful when you translate your ads into foreign languages. At the request of a seller whose property I listed, I had brochures for the listing translated into Russian because the seller would soon be traveling there. I used Google's translation tool, which provides a direct translation but doesn't account for linguistic slang or colloquialisms. Although the brochure looked impressive, I couldn't help worrying. "What if this says something offensive in Russian?"

My advice? As much as possible, make sure you're not turning your professional prose and image into something ridiculous to readers of a foreign language. The cost of hiring an expert in the language you are converting to might be worthwhile if you want to be certain of no translation faux pas.

VISITING AGENTS IN OTHER COUNTRIES

If you're taking a trip to Europe to tour Rome, for example, pack one of your suitcases full of brochures and marketing materials about your company, yourself, and your home market. Then visit real estate offices in Rome, interest agents there in what you offer, and possibly turn it into a business trip. (Confirm with your tax professional if you can deduct your expenses and legally make this journey a business trip.)

What better way to get international business than to visit real estate offices in foreign destinations? Agents all over the world have relationships with clients just as you do. They stay in touch just as you do. There's great potential for someone you encounter in an agent's office to say, "We're thinking about going to the U.S. and looking at real estate while we're there." Something might click! So you'd say, "The next time you visit the United States, come to Cape Cod." If you're talking to the agent, you'd say, "Send your clients to us in Cape Cod and we'll show them properties there."

When they arrive, schmooze with these international travelers; give them a boat ride, serve lobster rolls at lunch. Find great ways to connect and show them a good time!

JACK'S THEORY ON CLIMATE PATTERNS AND BUYERS

It's easy to assume that foreign buyers like to buy properties in warm climates, but that's not necessarily true. In my experience, foreign buyers tend to look for a geographic area that has a long season, whether it's warm or cold.

When they want to have winter recreation in a cold climate, they buy in Colorado, Utah, or Jackson Hole for the long ski season. The same goes if they want to enjoy a warm or hot climate. Then they buy in Florida or Arizona. So keep that in mind when reaching out to international buyers.

LUXURY AFFILIATION GROUPS

Through the National Association of Realtors®, look for luxury affiliation groups that include travel options in which groups of foreigners visit different real estate markets from time to time.

During one recent international industry event on the Cape, we opened one of our big multimillion-dollar houses for the group. To do that in your area, get in the pipeline to find out when these groups are coming. You can often find out through the National Association of Realtors®, Certified International Property Specialist Network (CIPS), and organizations such as the International Real Estate Federation (FIABCI).

It's a great opportunity to get to know international real estate agents by having them visit one of your listings. Imagine telling your sellers, "You know, twenty-five real estate agents from France and England are touring investment opportunities here. I want to host a gathering for them at your property." They'll be ecstatic!

CROSS MARKETING

I became friends with a manager who runs an office in Europe. Every time we publish our company magazine, I send him a box and ask him to display several copies in his office. I've actually had U.S. clients on vacation in London see our magazine display. How impressive.

We've also distributed our magazines in this country to real estate offices where lots of international people gather. Whether a prominent office in Palm Beach, Greenwich, or the Hamptons, people from Cape Cod see our magazine in the window of one of these offices and they're impressed.

The objective is to team up with another office in a location that complements yours and do cross marketing. Request their collateral material and tell them you want to display their materials because it enhances your image in your local marketplace. Besides, you're making friends and creating the potential for referrals, which is your ultimate goal.

CONNECTIONS AT CONVENTIONS

The National Association of Realtors® (NAR) annual conventions are the most direct and cost-effective ways to tap into international real estate. I can't think of any better way to get involved in the international marketplace than by going to the NAR convention every year. You'll find a whole section of the tradeshow called the International Pavilion where companies and agents from around the world set up their booths.

You can also attend receptions where you mingle and get to know foreign agents. You've found a captive audience for cross-marketing and you don't even have to leave the country! This opportunity provides a huge potential.

Also, if you're an agent, you can take the appropriate courses and you'll get to join the International Real Estate Federation (FIABCI) and the Certified International Property Specialist Network (CIPS Network), which are part of the National Association of Realtors® as mentioned.

The cross advantages of networking at NAR Conventions are huge, similar to the real estate version of the Epcot theme park. You can tour the world without ever leaving the convention trade floor and make invaluable connections. In a presentation I made at a recent NAR Convention in San Diego, about 10% of attendees came from outside the U.S.

When you meet and greet international buyers and agents, remember this: *Be your authentic self.* It's funny how some people think they need to take on an accent so they sound more international. Guess what? To an international buyer's ear, you already have an accent! So save yourself embarrassment and don't take on a fake one. You'll sound more international to them just by being who you are naturally.

18

MILLION$ IN
YOUR SPHERE

A "SPHERE OF INFLUENCE" IS DEFINED AS A GROUP OF INDIVIDUALS who can either do business with you directly or refer other people who can do business with you. Many agents believe that to be successful, it's important to have thousands of people in their sphere. The flaw here is that with too large a sphere, the task of staying in contact in a meaningful way becomes daunting.

I believe that a sphere of influence as small as 250 people can be highly effective if you're determined to succeed in high-end real estate. If each person in your sphere knows 250 people, then you have the potential to directly and indirectly influence 62,500 people. If you stay in the business long enough, this number can grow.

What's the ideal size of a sphere of influence? The answer depends on your answers to these questions: Can you truly maintain valuable relationships with 1,000 people? 10,000 people? What value is having a large number of people in your sphere if you can't maintain meaningful contact with them?

To drive home the value of your sphere of influence, use this sphere of influence certificate.

Fill in the name of a person in your sphere, then enter the value of a typical transaction this person is likely to refer to you. Also, what is the value of a transaction this person is likely to do directly with you? I entered these values on the form shown below using the name Dewey Listem with $2,000,000 as the likely transaction size referred by Mr. Listem.

Then estimate both the number of referrals this person is likely to refer over a 10-year period and how many times they're likely to do a transaction directly with you. Enter this number as well. You can see I estimated that Dewey would use me directly twice in 10 years and could likely send me two referrals a year during that same time.

I entered a commission rate of 3% and a split of 50% that, over 10 years, resulted in a total value of *$594,000* from this ONE member of my sphere.

While it's in printed form here, I also use it as an Excel spreadsheet so I can complete one for each person in my sphere if I desire. It usually takes two or three completed certificates to drive home the value of your sphere of influence. You can download one from www.jackcotton.com. Whatever your income goal, I suggest filling out sphere certificates so you have enough to derive double the income you desire. That way, if you are only 50% successful with your sphere, you can still hit your income target.

Keep in mind your goal is to develop a cadre of people who can refer business to you. That includes workers in the local boatyard and those in the golf pro shop or tennis shop. They usually have the direct-dial numbers of their CEO patrons and other high net worth individuals who live in your area. Including these service providers in your sphere of influence and bringing value to them can prove to be an important source of business.

Following is a list of occupations and fields that frequently cater to "people of means." Use it to jog your mind for names to add to your sphere. (If your mind needs even more jogging, look at Appendix B in the *Millionaire Next Door*.)

Advertising	Aerobics
Airline	Alarm Systems
Animal Health/Vet	Appraisers
Architects	Art Dealers

Sphere Certificate

Name:	Dewey Listem
Address:	423 Buried Treasure Lane
Address:	
City:	Amityville
State:	NZ Zip: 90210
Email:	Dewey.Listem@HOW

Average sales price from My Sphere referrals	$2,000,000
Average commission rate per side	3%
My split	50%
Average commission after splits	$27,000
Number of times this person will buy or sell with me over the next 10 years	2
Number of referrals this person will give me each year	2
Total value of this person over 10 years	**$594,000**
Average value of this person per year	**$59,400**

Artists	Athletics
Attorney	Au Pairs and Babysitters
Automobile	Banking
Bartenders	Boating
Bookkeeper	Carpet Cleaning
Chiropractors	Cleaners
Computer Techs	Consultants
Contractors	Cosmetics

Country Clubs
Dentists
Doctors
Firefighters
Florists
Furniture
Handymen
Health Club
Horses
Hotels
Investment Advisors
Jewelry
Limousine Service
Mechanics
Museums
Newspapers
Nutritionist
Orthodontists
Pedicurists
Personal Shoppers
Pharmacies
Plumbing
Pool Services
Property Management
Resorts
Secretaries
Software
Sporting Goods
Tailors
Tennis
Trainers
Universities
Wine
Yacht Charters

CPAs
Dermatologists
Engineers
Fishing Guides
Funds, Mutual and Hedge
Golf Pros
Hardware
Health Insurance
Hospitals
Insurance
Jet Ports
Landscapers
Management
Mortgage Bankers
Music
Nurses, Private Duty
Optometrists
Pediatricians
Pensions
Pets
Phones
Podiatrists
Printing
Rental/Agencies
Restaurant Staff
Skiing
Spas
Surgeons
Teachers
Theaters
Trash Removal
Wedding Planners
Yacht Brokers

FOUR WAYS TO BOND WITH THE WEALTHY

If you're a budding luxury real estate expert, your first plan of attack is to establish relationships with high net worth individuals as noted in previous chapters. A larger challenge is keeping them as permanent members in your evolving sphere of influence. Here are four tips to get high earners to stick close to you.

1. **Listen.** *You would think accomplished, high-achieving individuals would be idolized and adored by members of their family. Unfortunately, in many situations, no one in the family ever listens to the wealthy head of household. The kids often act with indifference and think it's cool to be aloof or in denial over their parent's success. Perhaps family jealousy is apparent, especially among siblings when one has been highly successful and the others have not. Whatever the situation, ask those you want to get to know their stories and sit back and listen with interest.*

   While some people might think doing this is a chore, in my 35 years of listening to stories, I have never been disappointed or bored. Learning about the road they took to their accomplishments fascinates me—and teaches me a great deal.

2. **Give recognition.** *Not only do many in the family not listen, they certainly don't offer recognition for each new level of achievement a wealthy family member might reach. So keep your eyes open, watch the business press and other media, and take time to recognize your clients at their important moments of achievement.*

   This can take the form of a simple note, card, or letter with an article clipping. You might even go to the extent of printing custom 12"× 15" backgrounds for laminating articles and magazine covers, which we've done for our clients. Why do this? People don't throw these away. And they sincerely appreciate getting the recognition.

3. ***Be you, be real.*** *Don't put on airs, fake accents, or pretend to be someone who you're not. Be competent in what you do; exude integrity; under promise and over deliver on the promises you make; always tell the truth. As mentioned earlier, people who have achieved lofty positions in society usually have the skill to detect insincerity. Never be insincere.*

4. ***Get adopted.*** *Well, this wishful-thinking piece of advice reflects my dream that one of my wealthy clients decides to have an eldest son and says, "Jack, we'd like to have you join the family. Could we adopt you? Here are the details of your trust fund. Why don't you pick one of the cars sitting in the garage and tell us where you'd like to live."*

Great fantasy, huh? Guess what. It's never happened and probably never will. Maybe it's because, in the adoption business, it's the young ones who get taken first.

Your Own Board of Directors

Examine the composition of the board of directors of any Fortune 500 corporation and you'll see that the individual directors come from a diverse background. The board of directors of a bank, for example, isn't made up of all bankers anymore than the board of directors of a computer company is made up entirely of computer people. A well-run successful corporation develops a depth and breadth of experience and knowledge through its board of directors.

While it might be beneficial to set up a mastermind group of fellow real estate agents from around the country, instead, consider setting up your own board of directors—people who have a variety of business backgrounds in your area. What if you met once a month with a banker, stock broker, financial planner, trust officer, CPA, builder, and yacht yard manager? The referrals back and forth and exchange of business ideas you'll gain can help build your business tremendously.

As always, apply the principle of giving before you expect to receive. Giving market information as well as referrals to fellow business professionals are highly valued and will likely result in referrals back to you.

Here's What to Say

Agents ask me what they should say when they talk to people within their sphere. I have two suggestions, one good and one great.

A good dialogue with someone within your sphere would be something like "Hello, Mrs. Bates, this is Jack Cotton of Luxury Realtors®. In thinking about your neighbors on Pineapple Island, who do you think will be the next ones to put their properties on the market?" Or "Thinking of your business associates at LuxCorp, who would be the next person likely to buy waterfront property here on the Cape?"

This approach gets the person in your sphere thinking about others in their network and might just result in referrals.

Alternatively, I like to ask for advice. Why? Because people from whom I've asked advice instantly think I'm smart for believing *they're* smart enough to give advice. With that in mind, I would use a call script such as, "Hello, Mr. Smith, this is Jack Cotton from Luxury Realtors®. I've just listed a fabulous property here on Egg Island. I need some advice. If you were me, how would you go about marketing this property?" In response, they don't normally send me to a certain web site, magazine, or publication in which to advertise the property. Nine times out of ten, they mention a well-connected person I should call.

Charity Events

"People of wealth" are known for being generous with their time and funds. As a result, they're constantly being invited to various charity events. A typical event features a cocktail reception, dinner, silent auction, and live auction.

As practitioners in the high-end real estate business, we are "hit up" to buy expensive ads in the program for various charity events. While this visibility has great potential and should never be ignored,

I can suggest better ways to both help the charity and remind high-end individuals of your expertise in the marketplace.

At several summer charity auctions in our market, we offer up a certificate for a sunset real estate tour of our marketplace by boat. The lucky bidder receives a 90-minute cruise with wine, cheese, shrimp cocktail, and commentary on the real estate market by noted waterfront property expert, Jack Cotton. In addition, we include a color booklet with maps that mark current offerings and recent sales.

Think about its impact: We value the certificate at a minimum of $500, making it rarely part of the silent auction. Rather, it's featured during the live auction. That means while hundreds of high net worth individuals are gathered at tables surrounding the stage, the auctioneer is happily embellishing your tour, touting the rare opportunity and value it brings to the lucky high bidder.

Throughout the event, you are featured as an expert in the area. When somebody actually bids up the certificate to hundreds of dollars, your credibility in the marketplace gets further cemented.

I make it a practice to ensure that the certificate sells for a certain amount and will enlist a family member, most often my wife, to bid on it to a certain level. Believe it or not, this gathers even more positive attention. We want them to think, "It must be great if his own wife is bidding." By the way, she has always been outbid in the end.

After offering the certificate, of course you have to make good on its promise. A common complaint of high bidders at charity auctions is that the purchased item isn't "as promised" during the event.

For that reason, if the certificate states a 60-minute boat tour, we make a point of going out for 90 minutes. If we talk about wine and cheese, we surprise them with shrimp cocktail, fine wine, Perrier, and so on. If there was ever a time to deliver more than is promised in the certificate, it's now.

The high bidder is frequently an investment banker or bank trust officer who uses the certificate to entertain clients. If you think about the high bidders at these events, they're people you absolutely want to impress.

Can you possibly think of anyone better to be with, one on one, for 60 to 90 minutes displaying your expertise in the marketplace? Here's an example of what one of our certificates says:

Leisurely Cruise
Around Oyster Harbors and the Three Bays

Enjoy a relaxing cruise around
Oyster Harbors, Osterville & Cotuit on Cape Cod.

Includes light refreshments,
color booklet with map and summaries of
recent sales and priceless commentary
on thewaterfront real estate market.

Approximately 90 minutes.

Good through 2009 season.

Six passenger maximum; weekdays preferred.
$550 Value

If you don't live in an area that's conducive to boating, use this same concept with other modes of transportation. What about a real estate tour via classic woody station wagon with a tailgate wine and cheese break overlooking a special vista at the conclusion of the tour? Or perhaps a helicopter or hot air balloon tour would be appropriate in your location. Maybe you collect antique fire trucks and can use one for the conveyance. The possibilities are limitless.

Ultimately, you succeed because you're offering something different—a valuable item that supports the charity financially and cements your image as an expert in the market.

19

THREE NEGOTIATION STRATEGIES NEEDED IN THE HIGH-END MARKET

It's easy to feel "outgunned" when negotiating with buyers and sellers of luxury real estate. After all, these folks are often doing billion-dollar deals as part of their daily activities. As expensive as luxury real estate can be, how do you compete on an even playing field with clients who regularly negotiate deals in the billions of dollars?

Over the years, I've read multiple books, listened to tapes, and attended seminars near and far on negotiation. Both Harvard Law School and the Massachusetts Institute of Technology (MIT), for example, offer fantastic summer programs in negotiation.

Based on everything I've learned and experienced over three decades in the real estate business, using the following three strategies can guide you through negotiations successfully:

1. Negotiate from a standpoint of preeminence.
2. Don't assume you know the needs of the other party in a negotiation.
3. Detach from the outcome.

Let's dissect each of these strategies so you know how they apply to high-end real estate.

STRIVE FOR PREEMINENCE

The dictionary defines *preeminent* as being above or before others; superior; surpassing; distinguished; peerless; supreme.

If you have acted on all the strategies and techniques laid out in this book, I guarantee you will obtain a level of preeminence in your market over time. You will become a leader in your marketplace— someone to be reckoned with. Even with poor negotiation abilities, the preeminent agent frequently prevails over the skilled but non-preeminent agent because people accede to those they perceive have power. Achieving preeminence leads to perceived power.

Becoming preeminent in your market is a journey and not necessarily a destination. If you expect to attain a level of preeminence in four to six weeks, you're not being realistic. On the other hand, you don't want to be looking at your business in a year realizing you've taken no steps toward your goal of being preeminent in your marketplace. I can assure you that most buyers and sellers of high-end real estate are preeminent in their professions. If you have any hope of holding your own, make this a primary goal as a luxury real estate expert. And if you've begun taking action on the ideas, techniques, and strategies outlined in this book, congratulations to you. You're on your way to preeminence.

MAKE NO ASSUMPTIONS

If I could name only one thing that gets people in trouble repeatedly, it's assuming.

When you assume you know the needs of another party, you often take off on a nonproductive course of action. The person you're negotiating with will dig in to hold a certain position and stay there. Negotiating from an unwavering position is often frustrating and fruitless. I can tell you that people who negotiate from a fixed position often find themselves in stalemate situations; they're in a terrible mood; they rarely obtain the outcome they seek.

In the examples we'll be discussing, a particular buyer takes the position of being willing to close only in the month of June. Another buyer will offer only 70% of the asking price. And a seller will only pay X% commission, no matter what.

As soon as one party in a negotiation gets stuck, the counterparty to the negotiation digs deeper into his or her position and the head-butting begins. What results? A stalemate.

Therefore, as the skilled luxury real estate negotiator, you must peel back the layers and look beyond the other's "stuck" position to understand (not assume) the person's true needs. In the case of the closing date in June, you may find out it's the date that coincides with the shipment of important furniture, art, or antiques. Therefore, you strive to find an alternative means of storing the items before the closing date to shift the buyer from his or her dug-in position.

When dealing with a buyer who will only pay a fixed percentage of the asking price, you may be required to peel even more layers off the metaphorical onion. You may discover that this buyer is insecure, has high ego needs, or has to get authorization from a third-party trustee. Perhaps this ego-driven person has the need to look intelligent and is incapable of negotiating what appears to be a great deal.

Once you fully understand the other person's needs, you can provide market evidence on the extraordinary value contained in this transaction. Perhaps you will present data on the cost to reproduce similar properties, assessment ratios, or other market-based evidence to allow this position-focused person to feel as if he or she has won.

You'll also encounter a seller who will not pay more than a certain percent in commission. It's no surprise that the higher the negotiations go in price, the more that seller wants to negotiate or reduce your fee. Here again, the seller's ego may be at the core, buoyed by a desire to show others he or she is a tough negotiator.

Probing often discerns the most salient need of the seller—to realize the highest price in the shortest amount of time with the least amount of aggravation. Sound familiar?

Many sellers, even in the high-end category, assume they can improve the bottom line in any transaction by reducing the agent's commission. Once you understand this perception, you can prepare to coach your seller that the best way to increase the bottom line is to increase the top line. How? Hire an expert in the sale of luxury real estate (you) who brings knowledge and experience in the market as well as a plan that creates a sense of urgency and competition among buyers. These result in the buyer desiring the property with the enthusiasm required to boost the seller's top line.

In every interaction, your goal as a luxury real estate expert should be to dig deep and find the "why behind the why." So you would ask, "Of course, Mr. and Mrs. Seller, you want to reduce the cost of selling your property. Why is that important to you?" And once you get this answer from the seller, you go one more level and ask, "Why is *that* important?" Or "what will that do for you and your family?"

As important as negotiating from need rather than position is assuming you know the needs of the counterparty to a negotiation. Be careful not to base your perceptions on your own beliefs and values.

For instance, if a buyer says he or she wants a property that offers complete privacy from neighbors, you (relying on your own belief or value system) might assume that the buyer wants a property with several acres. Further probing might lead to something different—like a special "jewel" of a property in an area where small lots are normal but homes are totally contained within walls and year-round landscaping gives them privacy. When you're not working from the same definitions as your buyers or sellers, it's easy to make incorrect assumptions. Always check them out!

WHAT WISH TOPS THE LIST?

One of my first clients gave me a laundry list of requirements for a property to buy—an antique sea-captain-type residence close to the water on at least an acre of land. Other wish-list features included high ceilings and a naturally finished wood staircase, which would be the focal point of the entry, and a barn on the property. Based on my conversations with the buyers, all these items seemed exceedingly important to them.

When the perfect property finally came on the market and I called to set up the inspection, I knew from the strange silence at the other end of the phone that something was amiss. They'd just purchased a house from someone else in another part of town and it had nothing in common with the description they'd given me of their ideal property.

Here's what I had failed to discern. While all the needs they had laid out were indeed important, their top priority was to get a great deal.

This situation happened many, many years ago. I bring it up today because it's arising with great frequency in our current strained economy. Many buyers have a burning need to be able to tell their friends, relatives, and associates that they got the most incredible deal on whatever they just purchased. Many times, this overshadows everything they laid out on their list of requirements.

Don't assume you know the needs of the other party nor assume that their needs are exactly as stated.

Detach from the Outcome

If you learn nothing else in negotiating, learn to detach from the outcome. Why? Because excessive attachment can allow your negotiation process to drift into position-based negotiating rather than need-based negotiating.

High net worth individuals need to know that you're not desperate to complete this deal. Whether you're on the listing side or the buying side of it, always be willing to walk away, and sometimes you'll have to.

Let me give an example of how I presented offers to a local builder of luxury second homes who had high ego needs and was a classic position negotiator. To make matters challenging, this particular builder-seller always wanted his properties to sell for more money than had ever been realized in the marketplace before. His aggressive pricing made it difficult to obtain an offer and when an offer did come in, his first reaction was expressed in ways that can't be stated in print.

I finally learned the concept of being detached from the outcome. This changed my whole approach to presenting offers to this builder. When an offer came in (always low because his prices were always high), I would simply say to him, "I received an offer on the property at Bay Road." Before he could utter a response, I would say, "I need your authorization to reject the offer." His response was, "Well, how much is the offer?" Then my response was, "It's low, and I need your authorization to reject it. I can't reject offers without your authorization." We would do two or three rounds of this when finally, in frustration, he'd scream at me, "How much is the offer?!"

So more often than not, when I stated the amount of the offer, he'd say, "Well, that's not as low as I thought. We can work with that." A counteroffer and different attitude followed. This meant he could say he was "saving a deal," which was great for his ego.

Asking for permission to reject the offer before actually disclosing its contents provides the ultimate signal of detachment from the outcome. You broadcast a message that says you're not trying to push the sellers into accepting something that you know is less than what they want (thus insulting their egos), even though it may be a fair offer in the current market.

Especially in a challenging market when sales can be far apart and few in number, it's compelling to get attached to the outcome. After all, it means money in your pocket. However, more than ever, this is the time to detach from the result. Just as a thoroughbred horse senses an inexperienced rider, high net worth individuals can sense your weakness and vulnerability.

In the End

With each of these three strategies of negotiation—build preeminence, don't make assumptions, practice detachment—understand that your personal power and reputation (as well as that of your counterparty) enhances your ability to reach a favorable result in any negotiation.

Your standing or stature in the transaction can't be ignored. Using one's stature or standing is a favorite tactic of the rich and powerful because it works. Who would have an easier time negotiating your marketing fee for a particular listing—a former president of the United States or a retired delivery truck driver?

Perception of power, prestige, and standing are huge factors when negotiating. Once your track record gets established and you become known in your marketplace, you'll find negotiations get easier. Not

186

easy, just *easier*. You may still get outgunned; you may still deal with people who typically negotiate transactions in the billions of dollars; but if you follow these strategies, you'll have more than a fighting chance.

In fact, they work equally well with buyers as with sellers. If a buyer makes an offer on a property that results in counteroffers and counter-counteroffers, you may find your transaction stalemated. At this point, I suggest saying to the buyer, "I'll keep looking for another property just as good as this. I'm happy to keep looking; I'm sure another one just as good will come on the market in the next several months."

When negotiating purchase price, never use position as the reason for either a buyer or a seller making his or her counteroffer. When you tell a buyer that the seller has to have $1.6 million because he or she is stuck there and $1.6 million is "the number," then you might as well kiss that transaction goodbye.

Always frame negotiations in the context of WIIFM (what's in it for me). In this example, a better way is to say that the seller requests $1.6 million based on marketplace knowledge, comparable sales, and competing properties currently available. In other words, talk about the market, not about the "stuck" position.

Charging Commissions

The question I'm asked often by agents is, "Do you need to cut fees when selling multimillion-dollar properties? Do people really pay your full rate in these cases?" My answer is a definite "yes."

To maintain integrity in the marketplace, it's unwise to charge different people different fees for the same service. After all, "people of means" travel in the same circles, discuss business with each other, and use one another for sounding boards when making big decisions. If you honestly think you can charge one person one amount and another person a different amount for the same service in the same market and not get found out, you're dreaming. Management by exception breeds disaster in the practice of any price range of real estate—and especially in high-end real estate.

I suggest you develop a policy or a fee structure and stick by it. For example, you can set commissions on properties of $1 million and less at X% and marketing fees on properties between $1 million and $5 million at Y%. Figure out what makes sense and write the details in a policy statement.

You may also decide to offer a different rate for different situations, such as listings referred by bank or trust officers. After all, these individuals can refer you a lot of business. They look like heroes when they can tell their clients they got the preeminent luxury specialist in the market for X% instead of Y%. It's still important to have a written policy stating that listings referred by bank and trust officers are X% instead of your standard Y%.

You may have a special fee for people doing a second or third transaction, for builders who list multiple properties with you, and so on. Simply put your fee schedule together on paper and stick to it.

CUTTING COMMISSIONS

Using the three strategies—preeminence, not assuming, and detachment from the outcome—is especially powerful in dealing with commission negotiations.

If you are the preeminent luxury specialist in your market, a certain percentage of people won't ever ask you to reduce your fee. Next, don't assume that the seller's goal is to net the highest possible price. That's not always true in high-end real estate, but make sure by asking. And detaching from the outcome means you're ready to walk away if people aren't willing to list on your terms at the fee you deserve.

I used to hear from our agents repeatedly that some agent at another company was undercutting us by X or Y points. They'd wring their hands with fear and trepidation, knowing they're getting ready for a listing appointment and everyone else in the marketplace is charging less. I was implored to match the deal.

Truthfully, commission cutting sends chills of excitement running down my spine. I'm not saying I love it when my company cuts commissions; rather, I love it when other companies in our markets charge less than we do. It confirms an important truth to me, which is this: *our competitors feel helpless to compete on any level except price.*

It means they believe they're not as good at negotiating and marketing. They know the value of their services and price accordingly. When you frame the unique selling propositions (USPs) discussed in Chapter 2 from a benefit quantifier proposition, most sellers will understand the value you bring to the transaction and agree to list at the fee you deserve.

As you may recall, during the second appointment in the listing process, I suggest you talk about four or five of your most important, cutting-edge USPs. To review, let's say one of your USPs is your negotiation experience and skill. The client (in a perpetual state of WIIFM) says, "So what? Why does it matter? What's in it for me?" Your benefit-focused reply is, "I average two to four points higher in a selling price of my sold listings than my competitors."

Then you repeat the process by discussing your staging checklists and market preparation abilities. I believe that my expertise in these areas will result in two to four points in the additional selling price. Then there's your luxury marketing plan. Is that not worth one or two points? Get the idea?

It's easy to get to a place of promising 10 to 12 points more in terms of potential selling price than your competition. I like to manage expectations of sellers by adding up the value of our USPs, which may equal 6 to 12 points, then in front of the seller, draw a line through the number written on a piece of paper and cut the amount in half.

Most of the time, we aim to sell at a one point difference in the marketing fee between ourselves and our competition. So if the value of our USPs will result in a selling price that is 4, 5, or 6 points higher, then it certainly makes sense to pay a one point higher marketing fee.

At times over the years, I have been tempted to give in to the agents in my company who wanted to reduce our commission fees to be more competitive in the marketplace. My main goal in doing this would be the delight I would get in saying, "I told you so."

You see, if we did reduce our fees, our competitors would be left with nothing more to do but reduce theirs even more. I always tell my agents that no matter what happens in the marketplace, most of the time, you are selling one point. Which point would you rather sell, the one between X and Y or the one between Y and Z?

Every strategy and tactic in this book leads to establishing your preeminence in the market. Combining that with the other two negotiating strategies in this chapter will aid you in holding on to the fee you deserve.

OBJECTING TO COMMISSIONS

In the course of an interaction with a potential seller, you'll find three times when commission objections tend to arise. They are:

1. During initial listing calls to the office. Here's the conversation: "Hello, this is Mr. Seller. I'm interested in having you come out and look at my house before I put it on the market. What do you charge for commission?"

2. During the listing presentation, often early on, when the seller asks, "What is your commission?"

3. Once an offer on the property is presented, even if the seller has agreed to pay your full fee, he or she may try to renegotiate by saying, "I had do come down on my price to make a deal, you should reduce your fee as well."

I could list lots of snappy, clever answers to their objections, but I hope you realize that receiving the compensation you deserve in a real estate transaction hinges on more than your answers to objections. Rather, it's part of the foundation you laid from the moment you first arrived on the seller's door to talk about listing the property.

You showed up on time looking and sounding professional, having done preliminary research on the property. Your file contained plans, deed, tax assessment information, plot plan, deed restrictions, and so on. You've already done more than what 85% of all the other agents working to list property would have done. Then, during your first meeting with the sellers, you delivered a prelisting package, which outlined the whole process you'd undertake to list their property and set their expectations. By this point, you've differentiated yourself from 90% of all the agents in the business.

You continued your appointment by asking questions that qualified their wants, needs, and desires as well as their timeframe and reason for moving. You went through the home room by room, measuring, dictating, taking copious notes on all aspects of the property. You talked about the laws of agency that apply to your market, most likely using a PowerPoint presentation. Then you filled out your staging checklist. You took copious notes of steps to be taken to enhance the home's value and shorten the marketing time. Overall, you cemented your perceived value with this client.

You teased the sellers with your work on the staging checklist, making clear to them that they won't receive the completed checklist until the listing contract is signed. You concluded the appointment without giving them a price until you do more research. Then you worked on a calculation to arrive at a price that would inspire them with confidence and that you'd willingly sign your name to.

You then returned to your office to work your CMA. You gathered the comparable information, which you were in a better position than ever to do having just visited the property. You adjusted the sale according to my seven elements of comparison discussed in Chapter 8 on pricing. You put everything together in a professional package to present to the sellers on your second appointment. At this point, you've done more than 97% of the agents who show up for a listing appointment.

On the second appointment, you continued your diagnosis, confirming the sellers' motivation and prescribing the action necessary to get the home or estate sold in the shortest time for the highest price with the least amount of aggravation. You gave a presentation that anticipated and disarmed their comments or objections. You presented your marketing plan. You identified and quantified three to five of your most valuable USPs. Once again, you teased your staging recommendations.

You presented your marketing plan, both in hardcopy and via PowerPoint, and reviewed the process you used to get the pricing processed to its current stage (approximately four in your seven-step process). At this time, you were ready to deal with any commission objections that might arise.

Again, your entire interaction has been so "above and beyond" anything the sellers have ever seen before that if objections arose at all, they were halfheartedly raised. Because you're detached from the outcome and are willing to walk away from this listing, you were able to get the contract signed. You stated that the price would be determined later at the full commission fee that you deserve.

I hope this scenario allows you to see how this process could apply to any negotiation as you carefully build a meaningful foundation to become a successful luxury real estate agent.

20

KEEP THE RICH AND FAMOUS COMING BACK

HAVE YOU REALIZED HOW REWARDING THE LONG, DETAILED PRO-cess for bringing high net worth individuals into your sphere of influence and finally into your customer base can be? Your next goal is to never have them leave your sphere once they opt in. They are too expensive to replace. You want to devote your efforts to bringing additional clients into your sphere, not replacing ones who've been lost.

The solution? Build a system for organized client follow-up.

Many professionals meet their clients once a year to review the area of their lives that they specialize in. For example, an accountant touches base with clients once a year for their financial tax situation. The attorney meets with clients once a year to discuss their estate or trust situation. And investment advisors meet once a year with their clients to review the status of their investments.

I recommend luxury real estate specialists follow this practice and prepare yearly value opinions of the property that clients purchased with you. We have covered the reasons why these updates are valuable. Your most important job is to anticipate client needs and prepare them, ideally once a year, without clients having to request them.

MORE VALUE

Some agents and companies plan and hold customer appreciation events. We held appreciation events years ago. When we had fewer people to stay in contact with, we had yearly lobster cookouts either during a boat cruise or at a shore-side location. As time went on and the numbers of attendees grew, we found them unwieldy, requiring a great deal of effort and planning that took away from other profit-generating activities. Again, it was a lot of fun and clients appreciated it, but the logistics were becoming a full-time job. We now send a card yearly letting our clients know a donation has been made to a local charity in their name.

In addition to the yearly review of a client's own property, monthly, or quarterly updates about the market in general is a perfect way to stay in touch and bring value to past clients. You can update them on the local market and give your opinion as to how national market trends compare with or affect the local market.

You can also join efforts with your affiliation marketing partners to offer valuable services, goods, or promotions as discussed in Chapter 10.

Again, whether or not your client is planning to get a new kitchen, or whatever the service or product, is irrelevant. The perception of and appreciation for added value that you bring to them doesn't go unnoticed. Following is a letter we've sent to past clients.

> Dear Past Client,
>
> During a recent visit to High End Furnishings, Inc. _____ (name), the owner/manager, made a special offer to my past clients. Enclosed is a certificate for $250 good for any purchase of $1,000 or more at the _____ store.
>
> We know how important the home is and hope that this gesture by High End Furnishings, Inc. will help make your retreat a little more warm and comfortable during this special season.
>
> On behalf of our entire team, I remain sincerely yours,
>
> Joe or Sally Agent

Along these lines, you are going to become a source of information for your high net worth buyers and sellers. Whether they need a landscaper, designer, architect, or builder, you need to be the person they call for the reference. While many of these practitioners will offer you referral fees or bonuses for referring clients, my advice is to politely decline the opportunity. I tell vendors who offer me these types of fees or bonuses to pass them along to my client in the form of a reduced price or even more superlative service. Referral fees from other real estate professionals are fine; referral fees from other businesses and professions in my opinion are not fine unless they're fully disclosed to all involved.

More than once, agents have come to me saying that a contractor, architect, or other vendor has offered them a referral fee for the client they brought into the vendor's practice. I find it difficult to say no to these requests repeatedly, so now I handle the situation by saying it's fine *as long as the fee is disclosed in writing to all parties involved.* Not once was anyone willing to make that disclosure, which tells me that it is not a good practice to engage in. You need to be the source of information and let it be known that you recommend the service providers based on their professionalism, quality, and reliability.

Lastly, at the conclusion of every transaction we send a written survey to the buyer and the seller in the transaction that used our services. This survey is designed to quantitatively evaluate the client's experience with our company. A sample form follows.

CLOSING QUESTIONNAIRE

How did you come to choose Dewey, Listem & Howe Realty? (*Please check all that apply.*)

☐ Past Client   ☐ Mailing
☐ Friend of Agent   ☐ Radio Ad
☐ Referral from Friend   ☐ Realtor® Referral
☐ DeweyListemHowe.com   ☐ Reputation
☐ Open House
☐ Advertising (Specify) _____
☐ Office/Walked-in _____
☐ Other _____

What did Dewey, Listem & Howe Realty do best in this transaction? _____

What, if anything, can we do to improve our services?

_____

What is the first thing that comes to mind when you think of Dewey, Listem & Howe Realty? _____

Please check one answer for each of the following questions:

How would you rate your satisfaction with your Dewey, Listem & Howe Realty Sales Agent?

☐ Excellent ☐ Good ☐ Fair ☐ Poor
☐ Other _____

How would you rate the quality of the Dewey, Listem & Howe Realty support staff?

☐ Excellent ☐ Good ☐ Fair ☐ Poor
☐ Other _____

How would you rate your overall experience with Dewey, Listem & Howe Realty?

☐ Excellent ☐ Good ☐ Fair ☐ Poor
☐ Other _____

Would you use Dewey, Listem & Howe Realty again?

☐ Yes ☐ No ☐ Other _____

Would you recommend Dewey, Listem & Howe Realty to Others?

☐ Yes ☐ No ☐ Other _____

May we use you as a reference?

☐ Yes ☐ No

May we publish your comments for testimonial purposes?

☐ Yes ☐ No

Who was your Agent?

Name: _____
Address: _____
Additional Comments: _____

_____

Note the fact that in addition to the quantitative responses, we give the client the ability to make a written comment or response. We also have two places to check off allowing us to use these accounts for testimonial and advertising purposes. Only a minute percentage of people who complete this survey do not give us permission to use their comments for testimonial purposes.

21

THE END IS JUST
THE BEGINNING

YOU'RE FAST BECOMING A LUXURY REAL ESTATE AGENT. EVEN BET-
ter, you have the know-how to deliver million-dollar service to everyone regardless of their price range.

Remember, how you portray yourself is arguably the biggest part of
becoming a successful luxury real estate agent. A lot of agents have
the misconception that to be successful in this endeavor, you have
to born rich and well-connected. If you were among them, I trust
this book has convinced you to "think again." If I can do it, you can.

Of course I'm not saying I'm the standard by which all others should
be judged. In the preceding pages, I tell you who I am, what I do, and
how my approach absolutely works in spite of the fact that I was
not born rich and well connected. I've built a successful business by
implementing the principles in this book.

I encourage you to perceive yourself as a high-end real estate agent,
and then take action. I can't promise everything will fall into place
immediately. It's a lot of work and success won't come overnight.

You now have the tools to become that expert. You can build the
confidence to convince the right people you're an expert and market
that expertise with savvy. Now it's time to move that expertise to
another level.

Five Steps to Move from Expert to Trusted Advisor

The ultimate goal for a luxury real estate agent is to become a trusted advisor. You want to be the person to whom high net worth individuals turn for advice on value, marketing strategies, and help for their friends who have real estate needs. You want to be someone they turn to like a parent or a spouse because you have completely earned their trust, and you must never, ever betray it.

The problem with real estate practice for agents in lower price ranges is the transience and short memories of clients. People in the middle price ranges don't have the constant need for expertise and advice. They aren't calling accountants and lawyers everyday as many high-end people do. Wealthy people worry about everything, especially value and taxes. Your goal is to be on their speed dial because you have moved from perceived expert to trusted advisor. Here are five steps to get there:

1. Think long term.

Success won't happen overnight; it must be planned, written out, and executed daily. Time will pass; in two years, you don't want to look back, having taken NO action, and wonder how far along in the process of becoming a trusted advisor you could have been.

Begin today. Make becoming a trusted advisor the foundation of your business long term and you will assure its continuity.

2. Tell the truth.

Would you be surprised if I told you that with rare exception, high net worth individuals have great BS detectors? Of course, exceptions always exist, but I can't make this point often enough: Rich people are not stupid!

Always tell the truth and don't try to put anything over on anyone, rich or poor. You should have one standard for everyone you deal with, and that is utmost integrity and truthfulness. I repeat: Treat everyone like a million dollars, no matter who they are.

CHAPTER TWENTY-ONE

3. THE QUESTION THAT ANSWERS ALL QUESTIONS—CLIENT FIRST.
Throughout your career, no matter the price point of your common transactions, you will at times arrive at a crossroads. When you find yourself in these situations, you will sometimes be conflicted about your course of action. In some of these instances, there may be a conflict between your self-interest and that of your client.

Example: You listed a $7 million house and lucky for you, you have two offers. One buyer is yours or that of an agent in your own company, and the other came from a competing office.

The offers are close to the same, or perhaps the offer from the competing agent's buyer is just a little better. What to do?

The answer to every question can be found in another question: "What is in the best interest of my client?" Ask this over and over again throughout the day. I guarantee it will guide you to the proper course of action in any situation.

We have been in this multiple-offer situation many times, and a good percentage of the outcomes favored the buyer of the competing company. The agent in my firm was never thrilled at these outcomes but understood and respected the answer to THE question.

You can take it a step further by asking several times a day, "Is the course of action I am about to take in the best interest of my client?" Whatever the question, the client always comes first. The rest will take care of itself.

4. ANTICIPATE THEIR NEEDS.
A client of mine who recently passed away owned a fine dining establishment in our town. He provided a great example of anticipating the needs of his clients.

One afternoon I happened to visit him one or two hours before the first diners would appear. I followed him through several small dining rooms of the restaurant as he tested each table to make sure there was no wiggle. He inspected each water glass to make sure there were no spots or stains or chips. Each butter dish had the insignia pointed straight up. If it didn't, he adjusted it on the spot.

The owner knew that you never get a second chance to make a good first impression. Anticipating and meeting clients' needs before they even know they have a need is service at the ultimate level.

Once diners appear at this restaurant, no one ever has to ask for a water or wine glass to be refilled or to ask for a sharper knife because the need is always anticipated.

As we work to become trusted advisors to the owners of luxury real estate in our market, we succeed by anticipating the needs of our clients.

As an example, tax time in the U.S. is April 15th every year. Months before that date, make sure an updated CMA arrives in your luxury property owners' mail, anticipating their need. If a property owner has recently purchased the property, copies of closing statements sent one or two months before April 15 is a clear signal that you are on top of that client's need.

Know the timeframe of tax events and anticipate assessed value updates, giving a heads-up to your client base.

If you live in a waterfront resort area such as I do in Cape Cod, automatically sending storm preparation tips and changes in conservation rules and regulations is another good way to anticipate client needs.

That said, by far the most important way you can anticipate the needs of your high-end clients is to automatically provide them with market data and updates. This is especially true if the property comes on the market and ultimately trades. They crave this information so send it before they have to ask.

Determine your clients' needs, anticipate them, and fulfill them before they actually become needs.

5. UNDER PROMISE AND OVER DELIVER.
Always deliver more than your clients expect.

The next time you stay at a Ritz Carlton, ask any staff member—whether it's the cleaning person, groundskeeper, or manager—for directions to the pool, spa, or some other part of the hotel. You will find they never simply give you directions to your desired destination; employees lead you personally to your ultimate destination. Ritz Carlton staff is trained to go the extra mile and deliver more than is expected. They own the problem until it is solved or passed on to another staffer with confirmation to the client.

Many times I get requests from my clients for valuation letters, as we have discussed in several sections of this book for various purposes. The client will say, "I just need something simple, a couple of sentences, a paragraph or two on a letterhead, to satisfy my accountant [lawyer, trust officer, etc]."

I always happily comply—and I can't think of a single time when I ever delivered just a one-page letter. I do a complete CMA with a summary letter, color photographs, maps, pictures, and arrows supporting documentation, and spreadsheets supporting my value conclusion. And if I promise it in three days, I deliver it in two. If I promise to mail it, I deliver it. If the client wanted one copy, I deliver two or three.

Moral of the story: Always, always deliver more than what is expected of you in any given situation.

Writing this book provided a valuable side benefit; it helped me to clarify my thinking after 36 years in this business. This book now serves as a reminder to make sure I'm walking my talk. It prompts these questions: "Am I doing everything I can to provide the best possible experience for my clients?" and "Am I doing what I tell other people to do in my book or in my talks or in my training?" It's a great reference and accountability tool for me, just as I hope it will be for you!

STARTING POINTS TO BUILD YOUR BUSINESS

First, build your base of knowledge of the particular market in which you want to work. Start constructing a two-year history of the market you've chosen. Obtain a map of wherever it is—the town, village, or section—and put all the little parcels, all the properties on the map so you begin to know it like the back of your hand.

Always do what you say you're going to do. Teach your clients about the services you can render them and make sure you exceed your promises. Conversely, learn their expectations of you. Surprise and delight your clients by going the extra mile.

The biggest snag you need to watch out for is becoming impatient because the title of this book is not *How to Become a Luxury Real Estate Agent in the Next Four Weeks.*

A hugely successful professional speaker named Patricia Fripp has given a talk called "How I Became an Overnight Success in Only 25 Years." How true that is! When people see me or any successful agent today, they tend to see me or the other agent in the context of where we are now. They generally don't see successful people in the context of all the work it took to get them where they are today.

It's a process. You'll get your share of scrapes and bruises. Instant success may happen and be prepared for it. In case that doesn't happen, however, this book presents a plan that, over the course of your career, will absolutely cement you as an expert and trusted advisor in your luxury market.

I wish I'd had a direct mentor starting out. I had several indirect mentors, some of whom were mentioned in this book. But when I started in business, I "knew everything." I was already an expert in my own mind and nobody could tell me anything. I just went out and started my company. Had I gone to work as an apprentice under one of the senior luxury practitioners in my market, I would have had a faster, shorter learning curve.

As a result, my company evolved as the Galapagos of real estate. Wealthy clients hugely influenced me, but their successes were in other endeavors of life, not in running a real estate business. At the same time, observing the great level of service at a Ritz Carlton and even the consistent service of a McDonald's had an impact. Still, my success would have developed faster if I'd just gone to work for someone else.

My suggestion for you? Set up a mentoring program with another agent in your marketplace, even in your company. Make it worth that person's while to be your mentor for a year or two by giving up a share of your commissions to speed up and fast-track your learning. Think of this commission sharing as tuition. It could turn out to be the best tuition money you have ever invested in yourself.

If you don't want to take the mentor route, find somebody in a noncompeting distant market and make them your accountability partner. Arrange to contact this mentor by phone and have a meeting once a week. That's an appointment that should be set in stone and used to hold each other accountable. As you execute each part of the plan as a result of reading this book, you can make sure that each one of you is doing what you're supposed to do. Sometimes, if you're on your own, it's easy to let something slide or do it halfway.

The Success Staircase

It winds. It spirals. It goes in one direction: up. It's time to continue to take those steps and keep going in that direction. It's time to put what you've learned into play. Of course, job one is to appear as the luxury real estate professional you are as well as give the highest caliber service to your clients.

However, along the way make sure to keep yourself in check. That means keep things in perspective, applying certain maxims repeated throughout this book: give them million-dollar service, under promise and over deliver, be yourself and don't put up any false fronts. Adhering to these principles ensures you'll stay on the up and up as you continue your ascent. Have a solid footing before moving on to the next step.

I always welcome comments and questions. Click onto www.JackCotton.com and drop me a line.

I leave you with every best wish for your success as a luxury real estate agent.

APPENDIX

SAMPLE COMPARABLE
SALES GRID NARRATIVE

THE FOLLOWING PARAGRAPHS EXPLAIN THE ADJUSTMENTS MADE on the sales comparison grid. This explanation is close to that which I use in an actual CMA. If this is new to you, imagine how new it is to a property owner. The more you explain it, the more you look like an expert.

The process for estimating the fair market value of a given piece of property is not all that complicated. We begin with the understanding of the definition of **fair market value**: *the price at which a property will change hands between a willing buying and willing seller, neither being under any compulsion to buy or sell, and both having reasonable knowledge of all the relevant facts.*

The next part of the process involves a complete and thorough inspection of the property, including room by room measurements and careful notation of all the features, systems, and amenities. This takes place during your first appointment at the subject property. Take special notice of any situations that could potentially cause a problem in marketing the property, such as hazardous materials like asbestos, underground oil tanks, or other items that might cause a problem for a potential buyer.

In the example, I find a well-constructed, 1920s vintage, Cape Cod-style home that contained approximately 4,567 square feet of living space on .77 acres of land. (These figures typically come from the town assessor's database.)

The dwelling has an attractive floor plan and it's been beautifully and lovingly maintained over the years. In addition to the main house, there's a separate, three-bedroom guest cottage. The main house enjoys water views, and a winding path from the west terrace leads to a deep-water dock that can accommodate up to three medium-sized boats.

The most reliable means of estimating the fair market value of a given piece of property is through the comparison of recent sales of similar properties. No two properties are exactly comparable and homes of this caliber tend to be unique. Nevertheless, this is the best method we have and comparisons are based on utility and usability rather than exacting feature-by-feature comparisons. In other words, I am not going to adjust for every half bath or bedroom, but on the main elements of comparison: privacy, views, location, utility, and usability.

I have looked at all the recent sales of similar properties and narrowed the field down to the three that require the least amount of adjustment when compared to the subject property. I find it more realistic to apply percentages to account for the differences between the comparables and the subject. For instance, certain areas of town, in my experience, typically realize sales prices of 10% to 20% higher than those properties located in the subject neighborhood.

The first comparable considered is located at 234 North Street in Seaville and sold in December of 2008. The sale occurred at $6,000,000 and because of the continued erosion of the marketplace between the closing date and the date of our evaluation, I made a 5%, or $300,000, negative adjustment to the price.

Sale number one had substantially more acreage than the subject at 2.23 acres. This resulted in substantially more privacy, requiring a 15% minus adjustment.

The subject dwelling contains 4,567 square feet compared to 5,123 square feet found in sale number one. The 12% larger square footage

Sales Comparison Grid
123 Sample Street
Cape Cod, MA

JC JACK COTTON

	SUBJECT	COMPARISON 1			COMPARISON 2			COMPARISON 3		
ADDRESS	123 Sample Street, Cape Cod, MA	234 North Street, Cape Cod, MA			567 West Street, Cape Cod, MA			890 South Street, Cape Cod, MA		
PRICE		$6,000,000			$7,450,000			$7,600,000		
CURRENT ASSESSMENT*	$5,580,700	107.5%			207.9%			156.0%		
SALES DATE		Nov-2008	-5.0%	($300,000)	Dec-2008	-5.0%	($372,500)	May-2008	-10.0%	($760,000)
LOT SIZE / PRIVACY	0.77	2.23 Acres	-15.0%	($900,000)	1.9 Acres	-10.0%	($745,000)	1.35 Acres	0.0%	$0
HOUSE SIZE (SQ FT)	4,567	5,123	12.2%		5,224	14.4%		8,562	85.1%	
COST PER SQ FT**	$300	$300		($166,800)	$300		($197,100)	$450		($1,707,750)
AGE	1920 Eff 2007	1920 eff 2000	0.0%	$0	1998 eff 2007	0.0%	$0	2002 eff new	-10.0%	($760,000)
FLOOR PLAN	Cape	Stucco	0.0%	$0	Cape	0.0%	$0	Cape	0.0%	$0
CONDITION	Excellent	Very Good	10.0%	$600,000	Excellent	0.0%	$0	Excellent	0.0%	$0
LOCATION	Sample Hood	Seaville	15.0%	$900,000	Goose harbor	-20.0%	($1,490,000)	Egg Island	10.0%	$760,000
VIEW	South Bay	North Bay	0.0%	$0	West Bay	0.0%	$0	North Bay	0.0%	$0
WATERFRONT	South Bay	North Bay	0.0%	$0	West Bay	0.0%	$0	North Bay	0.0%	$0
DOCK	"L" Shaped Deep Water	"L" Shape Deep	0.0%	$0	Interior	5.0%	$372,500	Interior	5.0%	$380,000
BEACH	Some Sand	na	5.0%	$300,000	na	5.0%	$372,500	North Bay	0.0%	$0
GARAGE	3 Attached–Living Space Above	na	5.0%	$300,000	3 Attached	0.0%	$0	3 Attached	0.0%	$0
BOATHOUSE		na	0.0%	$0	na	0.0%	$0	na	0.0%	$0
APARTMENT	Separate Guest Cottage	Guest Cottage	0.0%	$0	na	15.0%	$1,117,500	Permit	15.0%	$1,140,000
POOL	Gunite	Gunite	-1.0%	($60,000)	Gunite	-1.0%	($74,500)	Gunite	-1.0%	($76,000)
OTHER	Tennis Court	Yes	0.0%	$0	na	0.0%	$0	na	0.0%	$0
OTHER	Not Winterized	HVAC	-2.0%	($120,000)	HVAC	-2.0%	($149,000)	HVAC	-2.0%	($152,000)
OTHER			0.0%	$0		0.0%	$0		0.0%	$0
TOTAL ADJUSTMENT				$493,200			($1,165,600)			($1,175,750)
ADJUSTED PRICE as of	August 1, 2009 ($5m to $10M)			$6,493,200			$6,284,400			$6,424,250

* Average Price to Current Tax Assessment: 157%
** Market cost per square foot for comparable construction quality

Total Number of Competing Offerings 8

Number of Similar Sales in Past 12 Months 4

There is currently a 2.0 year supply of competing offerings.

at the market rate of $300 per square foot resulted in a minus adjustment of $166,800.

Sale number two was built around the same time as the subject and has been similarly maintained, requiring no adjustment. No adjustment was made for floor plan, view, water frontage, type, and quality of the dock and guest cottage. Sale number one had a guest cottage with a water view similar to that contained on the subject property.

Sale number one was in slightly inferior condition to the subject, requiring a 10% positive adjustment. I have also noticed that similar properties in the neighborhood where sale number one was located, Seaville, typically sell for about 15% less than those in the subject location. This 15% positive adjustment resulted in a $900,000 addition to the comparable number one price.

Sale number one had marsh frontage with no sand or beach area, which required a 5% positive adjustment. It also had a full HVAC system, pool, and tennis court, requiring negative adjustments as shown on the grid. Lastly, sale number one had no garage or living space above, requiring another $300,000 positive adjustment.

The net of these adjustments is $493,200, resulting in an adjusted sales price for sale number one of $6,493,200.

Sale number two took place at 567 West Street in Goose Harbor in October of 2008. Again, the erosion of the market between the sale date and our appraisal date required a 5% minus adjustment to the $7,450,000 sales price.

As with sale number one, sale number two had substantially more acreage than the subject although only marginally more privacy. This required a 10% minus adjustment or $745,000.

Sale number two had 5,224 square feet of living space which is 14.4% more than contained in the subject. When applying a market rate per square foot building cost of $300 per foot, we arrive at a further negative adjustment of $197,100. No adjustments are made for the similar age and condition of sale number two and the floor plan.

The largest adjustment of minus 20% was made for the difference in location between Goose Harbor and Sample Hood. It has been my experience that similar properties on Goose Harbor sell for approximately 20% more than those nearby but not on the Harbor.

Sale number two had a dock with a recently dredged channel, although it was still inferior, in my opinion, to that of the subject, requiring a 5% positive adjustment. Sale number two had a three-car garage attached, requiring no adjustment.

Lastly sale number two had a Gunite in-ground pool and complete HVAC system throughout the house, requiring minus 1% and 2% adjustments respectively.

The total adjustments for sale number two were $1,165,600, resulting in an adjusted sales price for sale number two of $6,284,400.

The last sale occurred in June of 2008 at 890 South Street in Egg Island for $7.6 million. In my opinion, there has been approximate 10% erosion in value in the 12 months since this sale, requiring a minus $760,000 adjustment. While sale number three has substantially more acreage than the subject at 1.35, privacy was similar, requiring no adjustment to be made.

The largest adjustment made on sale number three was for the 8,362 square feet of living space, which is almost 83% more than contained in the subject. The quality of construction for sale number three was of the highest level and quite frankly at a level rarely seen even in our marketplace. It's my opinion that the market value of this level of construction is $450 per square foot, which resulted in a negative adjustment of $1,707,750 to sale number three.

The level of maintenance and improvement to sale number three was also almost without equal. I made a minus 10% adjustment to account for this fact. No adjustment was made for floor plan, condition, water frontage, or views, or for the three-car attached garage.

In my opinion, Egg Island's location is inferior to that of the subject, requiring a 10% positive adjustment or $760,000. Also, sale number three had a seasonal dock, which is clearly inferior to that of the subject, requiring a 5% positive adjustment. Sale number three had no apartment or guest house although it did have a conservation permit to construct one. This resulted in a positive adjustment of 15%. Lastly, 1% and 2% minus adjustments were made respectively for the existence of a Gunite pool and complete HVAC system in sale number three.

Total adjustments for sale number three are $1,175,750, resulting in an adjusted sales price of $6,424,250.

I took the information a little bit further and calculated the average assessment ratio of these three comparable sales. They range from a low of 107.5% of assessment to a high of 207.9% of assessment. The average assessment ratios of the three comparable sales is 157%. The assessed value of the subject property is $3,981,100, which when applied to the 157% assessment ratio of the three comparables yields an "indication of value" of $6,250,000 (rounded).

Lastly, it was interesting to note that eight properties are currently on the market in the area priced between $5 million and $10 million, and four sales have occurred in the past twelve months. This leads to an absorption rate of approximately two years for the current inventory.

Considering all the information contained herein, in my opinion, the fair market value of the subject property as of August 15, 2009 is estimated to be $6,350,000.

Note: When doing a CMA, a qualified expert NEVER averages sales prices to arrive at an indication of fair market value. This statement may cause confusion because we often look at average sales prices, average assessment ratios, and so on. The distinction is that when looking at comparable sales, the qualified expert reconciles the market data into an indication of value.

Anyone can calculate an average. You could probably train a circus chimp to calculate an average. Your expertise as a luxury real estate specialist is in knowing the nuances of the market and therefore how much weight to put on each comparable. You may put most weight on one of the comparables because it was located two doors away and sold within the last thirty days. State that fact in your value opinion. You may want to mention the fact that you do not calculate average selling prices for comparables when discussing the CMA with your potential client.

APPENDIX

THE PRELISTING BOOK

My prelisting book, a component of the prelisting package, includes:

- my résumé and bio,
- a recent copy of our company magazine,
- press releases or reprints of news articles about me and/or my company,
- testimonials from previous clients, and
- bullet-point slicks featuring our company benefits.

I am a big-time fan of Shutterfly.com and love the quality of its hardcover photo books. I discuss the use of these photo books as property brochures later in Appendix B. In an effort to take my prelisting presentation to a new level, I created a hardcover version with all items noted above printed within one of these books.

Because the prelisting package is presented before clients even meet you, it should consist of a high-quality folder with your and/or your company's logo and contain your résumé, samples of marketing materials, and succinct bullet points describing your expertise, experience, and successes. I also include a separate cover letter on company stationery that I insert inside the front cover:

Dear Mr. and Mrs. Potential Seller,

Thank you for calling me regarding your possible interest in selling the above captioned property.

Prior to our first meeting, I thought it would be helpful for you to have some brief information on my qualifications and experience. In addition, this presentation will outline the process by which I will prepare for our appointments to discuss how I can be of service to you in maximizing the sale of your property.

Thank you again for the opportunity. I look forward to our meeting.

Sincerely,

Jack Cotton

Here is a rundown of what my prelisting package contains:

Cover: Keep it simple. I just use only my personal logo. With a short turnaround time, you could also use a photo of the subject property. The above letter is inserted inside the front cover.

First page (inside page right): My company logo and contact information. (Left inside cover is blank.)

Page two: This left-hand page has a photo of me in front of our office. Throughout the remainder of the book, the left-hand pages have photos or exhibits from my market area or from marketing plans. All written content is on right-hand pages.

Page three: Thank you for calling Jack Cotton regarding the potential sale of your property. This book is designed to provide background on Jack's experience and qualifications to market your property. It will also outline the process he will undertake to prepare for your appointment, and what you can expect during the appointment and afterward.

Page four: A local market photo is placed here such as a beach or other easy to recognize landmark from my market.

Page five: Prior to Our Appointment: Before meeting any potential seller/client, Jack will conduct basic research on your property, including but not limited to the following:

◆ Research and print any available GIS (Geographic Information Systems) plans and assessment data from the town.

- Conduct an online search of the Registry of Deeds and print:
  - Deed and/or Certificate of Title
  - Recorded Plan(s)
  - Deed Restrictions
  - Easements
  - Rights of First Refusal
  - Mortgage Information
- Conduct a general search of recent sales and competing offerings to be refined after the first appointment and inspection of the property.
- Begin process of drafting competitive market analysis for your property.

Page six: Local market photo.

Page seven: Our First Appointment.

Your first meeting with Jack will take as long as necessary to answer your questions and for him to gather sufficient information to prepare a detailed, written Opinion of Value that will be presented at the second appointment. Without a thorough gathering of information at your property, it is impossible to prepare a meaningful price opinion. Aside from getting to know one another, the initial appointment will include the following:

- Jack will consult with you as seller so that he can fully understand your goals and expectations in the potential offering of your property.
- Jack will discuss the laws of agency and ask you to sign a form confirming this discussion.
- You will conduct a tour of the property where you point out details and items of interest that only you, as owner, would be aware of.
- Jack will take a second walk-through of the property on his own to carefully measure all rooms and dictate a detailed room-by-room description.
- He will make notations on his ten-page Staging Checklist regarding items that can be undertaken to enhance market value and shorten time on market. This checklist will be completed and shared with you once the listing agreement is signed.

- Before leaving, Jack will take at least one exterior photo for his Marketing and Opinion of Value Report. Due to weather conditions and time of day, this may not be an optimal photo and will not be used in any marketing of the property once a listing agreement is signed.

Page eight: Local market photo.

Page nine: After First Meeting and Prior to Second Appointment

- The draft of the Competitive Market Analysis will be completed and the field of comparable sales and competing offerings will be narrowed based on Jack's inspection of your property.
- Certain properties will require detailed percentage adjustments to account for differences between your property and the recent sales.
- On a spreadsheet designed by Jack, percentage adjustments of the important elements of comparison will be made between your property and the recent sales to arrive at sales prices for the comparables that are more meaningful in the prediction of the selling price for your property.

Page ten: Samples of the spreadsheets used to adjust comparable sales to arrive at a price opinion for the subject property.

Page eleven: Second Appointment

- The second appointment ideally also takes place at the property, but it can take place over the telephone if necessary.
- Jack will present the marketing plan and his price opinion. Keep in mind that the price suggested in the Competitive Market Analysis is only the first step in deciding on the offering price of your property.
- You and Jack will discuss marketing and all of your questions will be answered. Initial agreement of the offering price will be made and kept confidential between you, the seller, and Jack. We may or may not actually leave the price out of our listing agreement.
- Lastly, Jack will review for you his Listing Evaluation Form. A score calculated from six factors that impact the sale of property will be calculated to predict the time required to find a buyer for your property.

Page twelve: Sample listing evaluation form

Page thirteen: The Pricing Process

- ❖ At the next available office meeting, Jack will describe your property to his fellow Company agents without any discussion of price.

- ❖ After the meeting, the pricing committee will tour your property with Jack. Members of the committee will share their opinion of value with Jack. Later that day, you and Jack will discuss the final offering price based on the recommendations of his fellow company agents and Jack's Market Analysis, and agree on an offering price. The listing will "go live" as soon after this meeting day as practical.

- ❖ Also during the meeting, a professional photographer will shoot as many inside and outside photos as necessary to fully capture the essence of your property. Jack will provide a checklist that will help prepare your home for photography.

Page fourteen: Local market photo

Page fifteen: Jack's bio

Page sixteen: Local market photo

Page seventeen: Jack's résumé

Page eighteen: Local market photo

Page nineteen: Last Page

Jack Cotton

FREE DOWNLOADS
of the spreadsheet tools featured in this book.

Location Adjustment Matrix	$ 30
Sales Adjustment Spreadsheet	$ 50
Sphere Certificate	$ 20
Total Value	$ 100

Yours free at www.JackCotton.com

Click Down Loads
Enter Password
Spreadsheets will be sent back as an email attachment

Free Downloads
$100 Value

Get the listing and pricing spreadsheets
described in this book.

See Pages 33, 76, 173, & 209

SHARE YOUR STORY

I hope you put the ideas and strategies in this book to use in your business starting today.

Send me your success stories, luxury real estate marketing ideas and comments.

jack@jackcotton.com

You never know, you might be included in a future book or program!